BOTSWANA
in Pictures

Alison Behnke

Twenty-First Century Books

Contents

Lerner Publishing Group, Inc., realizes that current information and statistics quickly become out of date. To extend the usefulness of the Visual Geography Series, we developed www.vgsbooks.com, a website offering links to up-to-date information, as well as in-depth material, on a wide variety of subjects. All the websites listed on www.vgsbooks.com have been carefully selected by researchers at Lerner Publishing Group, Inc. However, Lerner Publishing Group, Inc., is not responsible for the accuracy or suitability of the material on any website other than www.lernerbooks.com. It is recommended that students using the Internet be supervised by a parent or teacher. Links on www.vgsbooks.com will be regularly reviewed and updated as needed.

Website address: www.lernerbooks.

Twenty-First Century Books
A division of Lerner Publishing Group, Inc.
241 First Avenue North
Minneapolis, MN 55401 U.S.A.

web enhanced @ www.vgsbooks.com

Library of Congress Cataloging-in-Publication Data

Behnke, Alison.
    Botswana in pictures / by Alison Behnke.
        p.   cm. — (Visual geography series)
    Includes bibliographical references and index.
        ISBN 978-1-57505-953-2 (lib. bdg. : alk. paper)
        1. Botswana—Juvenile literature. 2. Botswana—Pictorial works—Juvenile literature. I. Title.
    DT2437.B673 2009
    968.83—dc22   2008027369

Manufactured in the United States of America
1 2 3 4 5 6 – BP – 14 13 12 11 10 09

INTRODUCTION

A landlocked country in southern Africa, Botswana is mostly semidesert and scrubland. For centuries a people called the San inhabited the area. They were nomads, who moved from place to place. The country is named after the Batswana people. This group dominates the modern nation. (The Batswana are distinct from the Botswanans, which refers to all the nation's citizens.)

Ancestors of the earliest Batswana began moving into the region from central Africa about two thousand years ago. In time they formed eight major kingdoms, each occupying its own territory. But when Europeans took interest in the region in the 1700s and 1800s, the Batswana were unable to keep them out. By 1895 Great Britain had claimed Batswana lands as part of its colonial African empire. In 1966 Botswana achieved independence from British authority.

Since gaining self-rule, Botswana has had only four presidents. Seretse Khama headed the government from 1966 until his death in 1980. Quett Masire, the vice president, succeeded Seretse Khama

as president. Masire was elected to the office in his own right in 1984 and again in 1989. Festus Mogae followed. In 2008 Ian Khama took office.

Botswana contains several ethnic and language groups. Most Botswanans are Batswana cattle herders and farmers. They speak a language called Setswana. By tradition, a small group of wealthy Batswana owns most of the cattle in Botswana. In the west and south dwell the San. They speak a language characterized by its clicking sounds.

Mining—especially diamond mining—is the foundation of modern Botswana's economy. With the aid of the national government, international corporations run Botswana's mining operations. Some of these groups are based in neighboring South Africa. After independence, Botswana was heavily dependent on South Africa. But Botswana's leaders have developed and diversified the country's economic ties. For example, Botswana has formed trade connections and organizations with other nations.

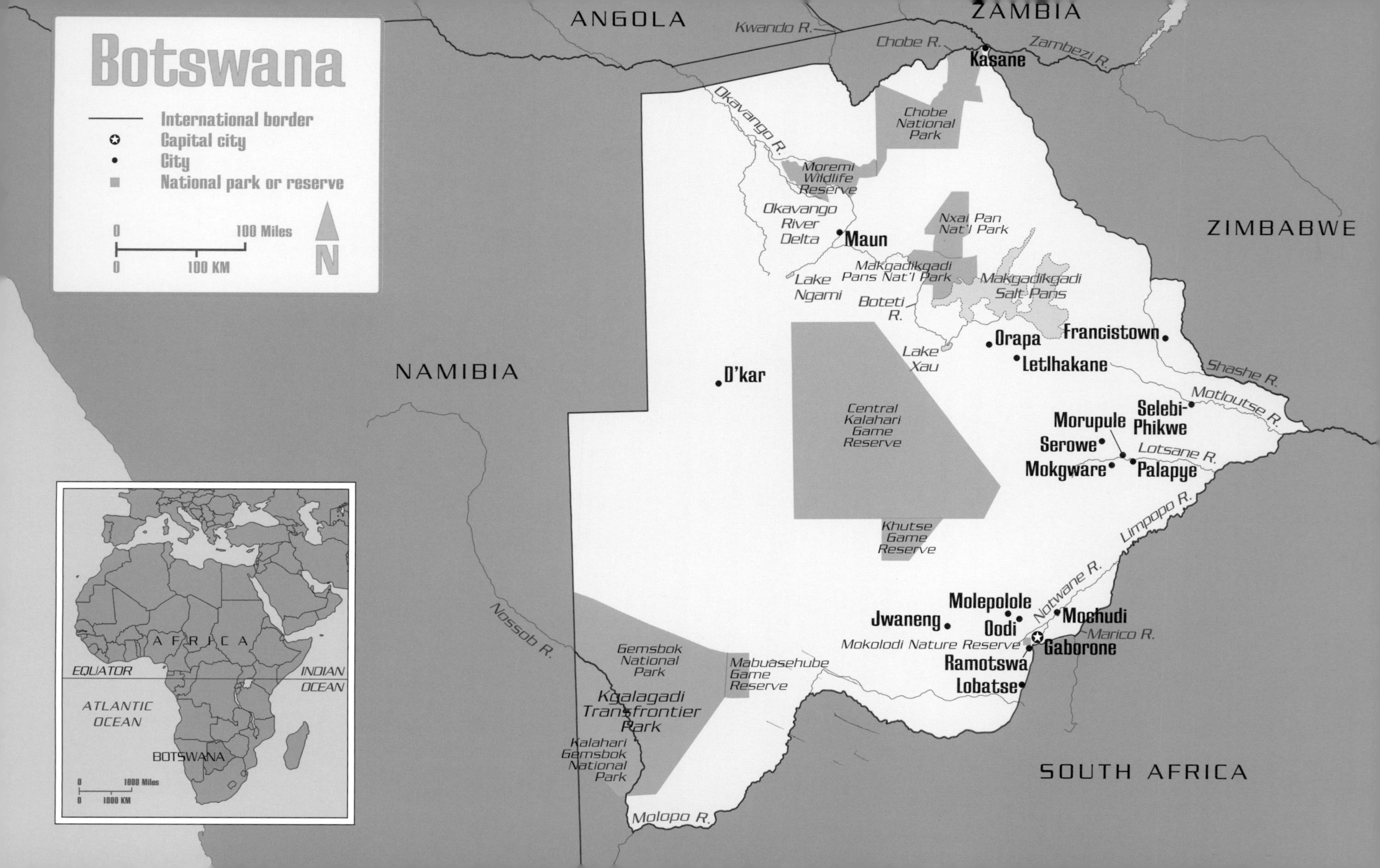
Botswana
International border
Capital city
City
National park or reserve
0
100 Miles
0
100 KM
N
ANGOLA
ZAMBIA
ZIMBABWE
NAMIBIA
SOUTH AFRICA
Kwando R.
Chobe R.
Zambezi R.
Kasane
Chobe National Park
Okavango R.
Moremi Wildlife Reserve
Okavango River Delta
Maun
Nxai Pan Nat'l Park
Makgadikgadi Pans Nat'l Park
Makgadikgadi Salt Pans
Lake Ngami
Boteti R.
Lake Xau
Orapa
Francistown
Letlhakane
Shashe R.
Motloutse R.
D'kar
Central Kalahari Game Reserve
Selebi-Phikwe
Morupule
Serowe
Lotsane R.
Mokgware
Palapye
Khutse Game Reserve
Limpopo R.
Notwane R.
Molepolole
Jwaneng
Oodi
Mochudi
Marico R.
Mokolodi Nature Reserve
Gaborone
Ramotswa
Lobatse
Nossob R.
Gemsbok National Park
Mabuasehube Game Reserve
Kgalagadi Transfrontier Park
Kalahari Gemsbok National Park
Molopo R.
AFRICA
EQUATOR
INDIAN OCEAN
ATLANTIC OCEAN
BOTSWANA
0
1000 Miles
0
1000 KM

Botswanans walk down a street in the capital city, Gaborone.

Botswana enjoys a stable government and a relatively high standard of living in comparison to many African nations. But wealth is unevenly distributed, and many people live in poverty. And beginning in the 1980s, the country's people faced a huge new challenge. The human immunodeficiency virus and acquired immunodeficiency syndrome (HIV/AIDS) is rampant in Botswana. Thousands of citizens die of this disease each year. These are daunting problems. But if the nation's people and leaders can address these issues, the coming decades may bring prosperity to more Botswanans.

THE LAND

Botswana lies in southern Africa. It is landlocked, meaning that it has no outlet to an ocean. With slightly more than 231,800 square miles (600,370 square kilometers) of territory, the nation is about the size of the U.S. state of Texas. To its east is Zimbabwe, and South Africa lies to the east and south. Namibia borders Botswana to the west. The Caprivi Strip—a long, narrow piece of Namibia's territory— stretches along Botswana's northern frontier. The nation also shares a short boundary with Zambia near the northern city of Kasane on the Zambezi River.

Topography

Most of Botswana consists of flat, elevated land with numerous low hills. The highest point in the country is Otse Mountain. This peak rises 4,886 feet (1,489 meters) above sea level in southeastern Botswana. Other uplands lie in the northwest, where the Tsodilo Hills break up the landscape with sharp, rocky outcroppings.

Botswana also contains three main topographical regions. The country's northwest is made up of a vast inland delta (the mouth of a river). The northeast holds flat, dry areas dominated by salt pans (areas of salt deposits). To the south lies the huge Kalahari Desert.

The Okavango River delta spreads over northwestern Botswana. This swampy area is created by the Okavango River and its branches. As the river flows southeastward from the nation of Angola, it carries huge amounts of sand and silt into the swampland. Covering more than 4,000 square miles (10,360 sq. km), the broad delta has agricultural potential because of its rich soil. But the region is too wet to farm. Some of the Okavango's water goes to marshy Lake Ngami. Water flowing from the Okavango also reaches the Boteti River, eventually entering Lake Xau and the Makgadikgadi Salt Pans in northeastern Botswana.

The Makgadikgadi Salt Pans are shallow depressions where small amounts of brackish (salty) water collect when the rains come. Thousands of years ago, these pans were the site of a large lake.

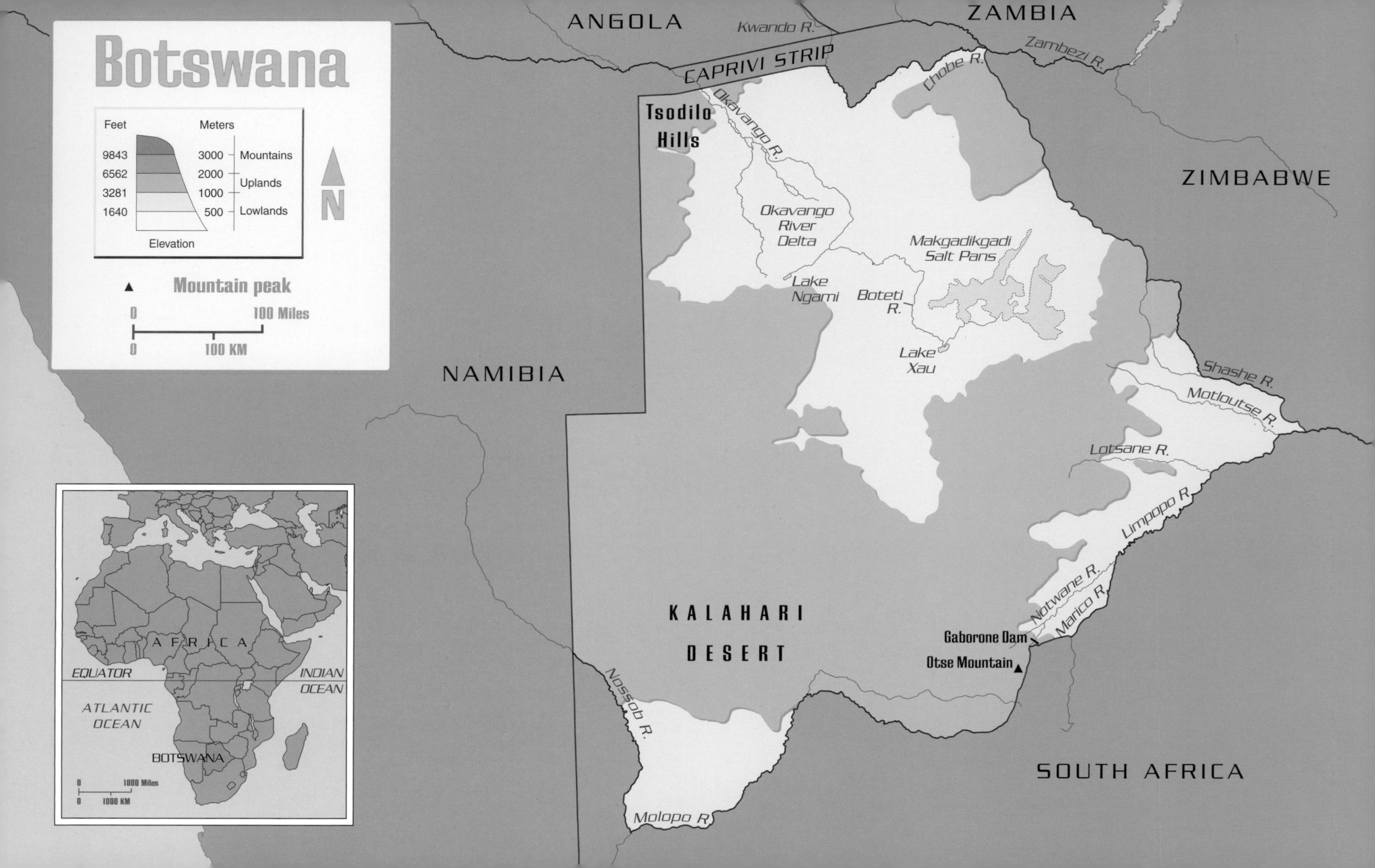
Botswana
Feet
Meters
9843
3000
Mountains
6562
2000
Uplands
3281
1000
1640
500
Lowlands
Elevation
N
Mountain peak
0
100 Miles
0
100 KM
ANGOLA
Kwando R.
ZAMBIA
Zambezi R.
CAPRIVI STRIP
Chobe R.
Tsodilo Hills
Okavango R.
ZIMBABWE
Okavango River Delta
Makgadikgadi Salt Pans
Lake Ngami
Boteti R.
Lake Xau
NAMIBIA
Shashe R.
Motloutse R.
Lotsane R.
Limpopo R.
Notwane R.
Marico R.
KALAHARI DESERT
Gaborone Dam
Otse Mountain
Nossob R.
Molopo R.
SOUTH AFRICA
AFRICA
EQUATOR
INDIAN OCEAN
ATLANTIC OCEAN
BOTSWANA
0
1000 Miles
0
1000 KM

A change in climate caused the lake to evaporate, leaving behind a salty deposit. Fed by the Okavango and Boteti rivers, the region changes from wetland to semiarid country with the seasons. In the dry period, water in the pans is sometimes only a few inches deep. The Makgadikgadi Salt Pans cover about 4,630 square miles (11,992 sq. km). They make up one of the largest salt pans in the world.

The Kalahari Desert dominates the southern two-thirds of Botswana. This vast desert makes up part of a large plateau that covers southern Africa. It stretches from Botswana into Namibia and South Africa. Across its territory, the Kalahari has an almost uniform altitude of about 3,000 to 3,300 feet (914 to 1,006 m). Only isolated pockets, such as the sand dunes of Botswana's southwestern corner, reflect true desert conditions. In these areas, little vegetation grows. Much of the rest of the Kalahari is covered with seasonal grasses. Small sections of the desert consist of rocky plains with occasional thorny shrubs. Although ancient waterways have dried up, underground water is close enough to the surface to support some plant life.

A WINDOW TO THE PAST

The Tsodilo Hills are noted for their multicolored stone and especially for hundreds of rock paintings dating from about four thousand years ago. These paintings show life and animals from Botswana's ancient history. In 2001 the hills became a United Nations Educational, Scientific and Cultural Organization (UNESCO) World Heritage Site. Being a World Heritage Site means that the hills and their paintings receive protection and conservation.

In the summer, the Makgadikgadi Salt Pans hold very little water.

▶ Rivers and Lakes

Water—and its absence—deeply influences the lives of Botswana's people and animals. Except for the Okavango River system, none of the nation's waterways flows throughout the year. Regional rivers carry surface water only during the rainy season.

Rising in Angola, the Okavango River travels southeastward for about 1,000 miles (1,609 km). Along the way, the Okavango forms a section of the Angola-Namibia border. The waterway then crosses the Caprivi Strip into Botswana. As it enters the nation's territory, the Okavango branches into a network of streams. The water from the river remains in Botswana and empties into the Okavango Delta.

Another important river in Botswana is the Limpopo. Like the Okavango, this waterway is about 1,000 miles (1,609 km) long. Its course separates the South African province of Transvaal from Botswana and Zimbabwe. Eventually, the Limpopo cuts through Mozambique. From there it flows into the Indian Ocean. Many Botswanans live near the fertile banks of the Limpopo and its branches, called tributaries.

In northern Botswana runs the Chobe River. This swampy, lower section of the Kwando River travels through Angola and Zambia and then along part of the Botswana-Namibia border. Eventually, it joins the Zambezi River. The Chobe flows through Chobe National Park—a protected wildlife area. The Shashe River runs along part of the border between Botswana and Zimbabwe. Shorter rivers, including the Motloutse, Lotsane, Marico, and Notwane, drain eastern Botswana's hilly

Two men boat down the Chobe River. The Chobe River forms part of the border between Botswana and Namibia.

land. This seasonally watered region contains all the nation's major cities, including the capital, Gaborone. Boreholes (deeply drilled wells) in this region reach underground water to serve the needs of these urban areas.

In the Kalahari, some rivers appear during the wet season. The Nossob, which begins in Namibia and forms part of the Namibia-Botswana border in the southwest, is one such waterway. The Molopo River also runs through the Kalahari seasonally, flowing along a large stretch of Botswana's boundary with South Africa.

Botswana has few lakes. One of the best known is Lake Ngami, located in the northwest. While local fishers and other residents had long known of this shallow lake, the first European to see it was David Livingstone. This British missionary and explorer reached Ngami in 1849. Scientists estimate that in the ancient past it may have been almost 700 square miles (1,813 sq. km) in area. But it was much smaller when Livingstone saw it. During droughts—periods of extremely low rainfall—the lake can dry up completely. The lake has disappeared in this way several times over the centuries and probably will again in the future.

Other bodies of water in Botswana include Lake Xau. This salty, marshy lake lies near the center of Botswana, just southwest of the Makgadikgadi Salt Pans. And in the Kalahari Desert, water collects in shallow lakes that form immediately after a rainfall.

◐ Climate

Botswana is situated in the Southern Hemisphere, south of the equator (the imaginary line that marks the halfway point between the North Pole and the South Pole). Therefore, winter in the nation occurs between May and September. Summer takes place between October and April. The nation's location in the subtropical belt of the African continent makes average daytime temperatures high. But Botswana's average altitude of approximately 3,300 feet (1,006 m) also keeps temperatures quite cool at night.

The warmest places in Botswana are in the north at the cities of Kasane and Maun. The hottest part of the year falls between October and April. Temperatures during this period can rise to 100°F (38°C) in the middle of the day. In the coldest months of June and July, temperatures often fall below freezing (32°F, or 0°C) at night. Frosts frequently occur during this season. In August, hot, dry winds carry sand from the Kalahari Desert across the country.

Rain falls unevenly in Botswana. The nation's wettest region is the north, where annual precipitation averages from 17 to 25 inches (43 to 64 centimeters). Rainfall decreases across the rest of the country. The Kalahari Desert usually receives no more than 9 inches (23 cm) of rain—and often much less—each year.

Rainfall and the availability of water in a dry land have always been critical to Botswana's people. In fact, the name of the country's unit of money—the pula—means "rain" in the Batswana language Setswana. "Let there be rain" is a formal greeting between Botswanans.

Rainfall in Botswana also depends on the season. While the Kalahari is dry most of the year, other parts of the nation experience rainy and dry periods. The wettest part of the year is usually January and February. The dry season in most of Botswana begins around May and lasts into November. In addition, the entire country is subject to periodic droughts. Serious droughts struck the nation in the 1960s and the 1980s.

◎ Flora and Fauna

Botswana's vegetation depends on regional rainfall. For example, the drier parts of the Kalahari feature shrub grasslands, while the wetter areas contain trees. The moist northeastern part of the nation supports tree savanna (a mixture of trees and grass). In addition, small areas of Botswana are forested, such as the banks of the Chobe River. Acacias are the most common tree species in the country. Bloodwood and teak trees grow there as well.

Baobab trees also grow in Botswana. Baobabs have short but massively thick trunks. They can live to be hundreds of years old. One

Two common trees in Botswana are the acacia *(left)* and the baobab *(right)*.

stand of the trees is in northern Botswana's Nxai Pan National Park. It is often called Baines' Baobabs because a British artist, Thomas Baines, painted it in 1862. The group of seven trees—also known as the Sleeping Sisters—remains an attraction for visitors to modern Botswana. It looks almost the way Baines depicted it more than a century ago.

The Okavango Delta abounds with birds and mammals. Animal life in this rich region includes zebras (the national animal), elephants, wildebeests, giraffes, hippopotamuses, and kudu (antelope with spirally twisted horns). Other kinds of antelope—as well as lions, leopards, and crocodiles—also live in the country. Poisonous snakes, such as cobras and puff adders, are quite common, as are many varieties of scorpions, spiders, and termites.

Many bird species reside in Botswana, including ostriches, pelicans, flamingos, and bustards (large birds that live in Botswana's grasslands). Another winged resident is the Cape Griffon vulture. These scavengers are among the largest African vultures, with an average wingspan of almost 8 feet (2.4 m).

VERY LARGE NEIGHBORS

Botswana is home to more elephants *(below)* than any other nation in the world. Experts estimate that more than 120,000 of the huge animals roam Botswana's territory. Because elephants have been endangered in the past, this large population represents a victory. But it also causes problems. For example, farmers complain that the elephants damage crops.

Above: **Kudu** drink from a watering hole. *Inset:* A **hippopotamus** cools off in the Okavango Delta.

But these vultures are endangered, due to a variety of mostly human-caused threats. For example, some birds have electrocuted themselves on electric lines, while others have had their breeding sites and nests disturbed by humans.

The main types of fish in Botswana's waters include tilapia, pike, tiger fish, and catfish. They live mostly in the Chobe and Okavango rivers.

Natural Resources and Environmental Challenges

Although many of Botswana's natural resources are underdeveloped, several valuable materials exist there. Nickel, cobalt, and copper are found in the northeast, near the cities of Francistown and Selebi-Phikwe. Supplies of coal, silver, iron ore, soda ash (used in producing glass, chemicals, and other materials), and manganese (used in iron and steel production) have also been found.

But Botswana's most valuable resource is its gem-quality diamonds, discovered in the late 1960s. Major diamond mines in Botswana include the east central Orapa and Letlhakane mines, as well as at Jwaneng, west of Gaborone. Botswana earns a large export income from its diamond industry, which the government and a South African company run jointly.

Another of Botswana's great resources is its rich biodiversity (range of wildlife). But tourism, pollution, and hunting can all threaten the nation's animals. To address this problem, the government has established several wildlife reserves across the country. Among the biggest national parks in Botswana are Chobe in the north and Gemsbok (part of the Kgalagadi Transfrontier Park) in the southwest. Laws also protect animals on reserves, such as the Central Kalahari Game Reserve, the Makgadikgadi Pans National Park, and the Moremi Wildlife Reserve in the Okavango Delta. In addition, the government carefully monitors about forty hunting blocks, where hunters may shoot small quantities of game. Authorities issue only a limited number of shooting permits each year.

Botswana also struggles with other environmental troubles, including water and air pollution, and problems with waste management. Botswana's government has created many programs and laws to tackle these issues. The nation has also received some help from international organizations. While the nation still faces significant challenges, it is improving its environmental situation.

A herd of zebras runs across the Makgadikgadi Pans National Park.

◉ Cities and Towns

Most Botswanans live in the eastern one-third of the country. Just less than half of the nation's people inhabit rural areas. Cities and towns have grown rapidly since the late twentieth century, mostly because villagers have moved to urban areas in search of jobs.

Botswana's largest city is the capital, Gaborone, located in the southeast. This fast-growing settlement became the nation's major administrative center after Botswana's independence in 1966. The carefully planned city is home to about 200,000 residents, who live in modern buildings and neighborhoods. A broad street called the Mall cuts through the middle of the capital, and government structures lie at both ends of this main thoroughfare. The government of Botswana is Gaborone's chief employer. The city is also home to museums, many businesses, and an airport.

Francistown is the nation's second-largest city, with an estimated population of about 83,000. As many as 113,000 people may live in the greater Francistown area. (The government has not officially counted its population since 2001, and population estimates of many cities vary widely.) Lying in northeastern Botswana near the Zimbabwean border, the city developed from a minor gold-rush town into a commercial center. It remains a mining capital, with reserves of copper, nickel, and cobalt. The city also serves as the starting point for many tourist journeys into the nation's wildlife parks.

Molepolole, with approximately 55,500 to 65,000 people, is another major population center. Lying about 30 miles (48 km) northwest of

Almost half of Botswana's people live in **rural areas** like this one.

Downtown Gaborone features highrise buildings and wide streets, including the Mall.

Gaborone, it was a historic capital for the Bakwena ethnic group. Many travelers into the Kalahari set off from Molepolole.

Selebi-Phikwe grew rapidly from a small agricultural village into a mining community of more than 50,000. Located in east central Botswana, Selebi-Phikwe is linked to Gaborone by railways and roads. Comfortable residential areas surround Selebi-Phikwe. Mines, an ore-processing plant, an electrical factory, and other industrial sites are on the outskirts.

Another important city is Serowe. Lying about 50 miles (80 km) southwest of Selebi-Phikwe, the city has a population of more than 42,000 (some estimates are as high as 90,000). Serowe is the chief city of the Bangwato people. This Batswana group once controlled the largest kingdom in the country. In modern times, Serowe still follows the layout of a traditional village, with many round dwellings and a central meeting place.

Lobatse (population about 30,000) in southeastern Botswana is the hub of the nation's cattle-processing industry. The city's slaughterhouse is one of the largest plants of its kind in Africa. Most local businesses involve or support the livestock trade. Craft industries also exist. In addition, Lobatse serves as the site of Botswana's supreme court.

Visit www.vgsbooks.com for links to websites with additional information about the landscape, climate, and cities of Botswana.

HISTORY AND GOVERNMENT

Historians believe that humans have lived in the area that became Botswana for many thousands of years. Archaeological evidence shows early settlements and migration in the area. These findings suggest that the nation had an important role in southern Africa's ancient history.

As long as two million years ago, ancestors of early humans lived in Botswana. By about fifty thousand years ago, the region's inhabitants looked very much like modern human beings. The early residents of Botswana used stone tools, hunted game, and gathered plants. Cave paintings found in the area depict antelope and hippos. These animals must have been some of the creatures that lived among the hunting and gathering peoples.

◉ Early Inhabitants

From these original communities developed the San and the Khoikhoi peoples. The descendants of these early peoples still

dwell in Botswana. (Europeans later named the San "Bushmen" and called the Khoikhoi "Hottentots.") About three thousand years ago, these two groups were well established throughout southern Africa. Various subgroups—sometimes called bands—competed for the area's water and food.

The San were skilled hunters. They used light bows and poison-tipped arrows to kill their prey. San women gathered plants, while San men provided meat and fish. The Khoikhoi hunted and gathered as well. But unlike the San, they also kept livestock, primarily sheep and cattle. The San lived mostly in the southwest and northwest. The Khoikhoi occupied the center and north of the country.

Over time, the ways of the San and Khoikhoi began to differ mark-edly. This split may have been a result of the Khoikhoi's ownership of livestock. The San continued to hunt, gather, and live a nomadic life in small groupings. The Khoikhoi became herders of cattle and formed permanent villages.

Most experts believe that the San are the oldest ethnic group in sub-Saharan Africa. Their ancestors may have lived in this region for at least twenty thousand years and possibly more than thirty thousand.

○ Bantu Migration

After centuries of competing for game, the San and the Khoikhoi encountered other ethnic groups. Sometime before A.D. 100, Bantu-speaking peoples began a gradual, southward migration from central Africa. These incoming settlers grew crops and used iron tools. Eventually, some Bantu speakers intermarried with the San and the Khoikhoi. The new families set up small agricultural villages. In Botswana, farming communities existed near the site of Francistown, along the Chobe River, and in the Tsodilo Hills.

The arrival of the Bantu-speaking groups altered the way of life in Botswana. The newcomers brought different tools and farming methods. These changes allowed the area to support a greater number of people. Populations grew, and village life became more structured.

As a result of the migration of the Bantu speakers, knowledge of iron and smelting (an ore-melting process) became widespread. Between A.D. 1000 and 1250, mining sites around the region rose in number. In addition, cattle herds and crop yields increased, helping local populations improve their food supply. People in Botswana's region began trading with related ethnic groups in other parts of southern Africa. Copper, iron, gold, and ivory were the main trade items.

Using overland routes, traders took goods from landlocked Botswana to sites with access to the sea. These trading centers flourished by selling metals and ivory from Botswana and elsewhere.

○ Batswana Subgroups Form

Trading profits and abundant crops strengthened the early Bantu-speaking groups. They began to form small, loosely organized communities. These groupings extended over a wide area in southern Africa. By the early fourteenth century, the communities had become more stable. In Botswana most people lived in the north and east, near plentiful water sources. Others lived outside Botswana along the southern African coasts.

As the number of people grew, it became more difficult to shelter and feed these large populations. As a result, extended families split off from one another. They established independent subgroups but often kept ties through marriage. During certain periods, droughts also caused communities to break up into smaller units. These groups spread over larger areas in search of food and water.

By about 1300, most of the Bantu-speaking peoples in Botswana belonged to the Batswana. This group spoke Setswana, a member of the Bantu family of languages. The Batswana further split into eight major subgroups, called clans. These clans included the Bangwato, the Barolong, the Bakwena, and the Bakgatla.

Social Organization

Each of the Batswana groups supported a strong social structure. The head of a clan was its *kgosi*, or king. His son or another male relative inherited the *bogosi* (kingship) from him. The kgosi was not an all-powerful ruler. An assembly of adult males—called the *kgotla*—helped the king decide matters of common interest.

People related to the ruler came next in the social organization. They formed the upper class of clan society. Ranked in the middle were members of nonroyal families. They were often part of the group's hunting parties, or *letsholo*. At the bottom were non-Batswana peoples, including the San and the Khoikhoi. These people did most of the manual labor.

Economic activities in Batswana kingdoms focused on providing basics such as food, clothing, and housing. Herding livestock, farming small plots of land, hunting animals, and gathering food were common pursuits. Agriculture was not always successful because of the limited rain. Permanent communities grew up near reliable supplies of water. These settlements were centers for political and social life.

Batswana kings and the heads of powerful families owned large cattle herds. In addition, they collected tribute (payment) from weaker groups. They demanded these tributes mostly from non-Batswana peoples such as the Bayei and Bakalanga. These forced payments caused resentment between groups.

Emerging Conflicts

After 1600 more Batswana clans moved northward and westward from southern Africa into the open spaces of Botswana. With their arrival, areas of settlement and trade contacts expanded.

Meanwhile, merchants from the Netherlands were exploring and settling the region. In the early seventeenth century, these Dutch arrivals established a foothold at Africa's southern tip—a place called the Cape of Good Hope. Eventually, they set up the Cape Colony. By 1652 Dutch livestock farmers, known as the Boers, had joined the Cape Colony. They claimed ownership of large expanses of African land. This activity brought them into conflict with the Khoikhoi and the San. Both African groups regarded the animals that the Dutch herded as wild and therefore as fair game for hunting. The Dutch disagreed and vowed to wipe out the African hunters. In the seventeenth and eighteenth centuries, the Dutch killed or enslaved most of the Khoikhoi. After decades of conflict that drastically reduced their numbers, the San fled to the Kalahari Desert—where white settlers were unlikely to follow.

In time, the Boers also fought with many different Bantu-speaking groups about land. This warfare in what eventually became South Africa pushed more peoples toward Botswana. In the 1600s and 1700s, Botswana's population and area of settlement increased, mainly through immigration.

The Boers' ongoing land claims in the south caused tensions among the Batswana, as well as among other Africans in the region. In former times, there had been enough land to satisfy the grazing and farming needs of all groups. Because of Boer activities, however, African groups began to fight one another for the limited pastureland. As a result of this conflict, one powerful ethnic group came to dominate southern Africa. That group was the Zulu.

In about 1815, a Zulu warrior-king named Shaka organized his followers into an army. The Zulu soon took over the lands of nearby African peoples, pushing many Batswana and related clans northward and westward. Some of these refugees regrouped to fight back. Others completely left the area to escape the fighting, and many of them ended up in Botswana. This forced migration caused by Zulu warfare was called the *difaqane*. In the 1820s and into the 1830s, the difaqane relocated many African groups.

◉ British Missionaries Arrive

A new foreign group was also making their presence felt in the 1820s. Christian missionaries (religious teachers and workers) ventured into the lands of the Batswana. They were members of the London Missionary Society, a Protestant organization based in Great Britain. Robert Moffat was among the earliest missionaries to visit the area. However, his attempts to convert Batswana clans from traditional religions to Christianity were not very successful.

Moffat's son-in-law, David Livingstone, set up a missionary station among the Bakwena near present-day Molepolole. He was more successful than Moffat in his efforts. Because of Livingstone's work, the Bakwena kgosi Sechele I became a

David Livingstone

This 1837 U.S. engraving shows Afrikaners making the **Great Trek.**

Christian in 1848. Livingstone also contacted other Batswana clans. They gave him a warm welcome. But this friendliness stemmed more from a hope of getting European weapons than from an enthusiasm for Christianity. Besides their religious purpose, British missionaries also wanted to explore unmapped areas of the continent and to encourage Africans to trade with Britain.

By the mid-1800s, the Batswana came into increasing contact with various European communities. This exposure was a result of warfare, trade, and missionary work. The Batswana bought European rifles to fight the descendants of the Boers—African-born whites called Afrikaners. The missionaries introduced European farming techniques and tools. These changes allowed powerful Batswana families to increase their harvests. They then traded the surplus crops for more European products, especially guns. Many Afrikaners also made treks—migrations deeper into the African interior. This movement began to restrict African settlements.

Colonial Rule

By the 1860s, Afrikaners were widening their territorial claims in Africa. One reason was the discovery of precious minerals—including gold. These finds made areas of the Transvaal, South Africa, very valuable to the Afrikaners, as well as to British investors.

The British and the Afrikaners soon clashed over control of the gold and diamond deposits. These conflicts temporarily distracted the Afrikaners from warfare with the Africans. As a result, the Batswana gained greater stability. Scattered groups formed larger units, and these new kingdoms obtained more guns to protect their lands from Afrikaner expansion.

In the 1870s, the threat of open hostilities between the Afrikaners and the Batswana increased. Afrikaners regarded all land north, east, and west of the Transvaal as their property. But the Batswana groups who lived in these regions rejected the Europeans' territorial claims. One African ruler—the Bangwato king Khama III—asked the British for protection against the Afrikaners, but the British refused his request.

Meanwhile, other European powers, particularly Germany, had grown interested in colonizing southern Africa. Britain saw German influence in Africa as a threat to British trade. By 1884 Germany had taken over South-West Africa (present-day Namibia). In 1885, to maintain their own control in the region, the British told the Batswana that their lands were under British protection. The Europeans had dubbed this area Bechuanaland.

The British made the region south of the Molopo River a colonial territory, called British Bechuanaland. The area north of the river was also under British protection and was named the Bechuanaland Protectorate. Although the British government controlled the protectorate, the British did not claim legal ownership of the land. But the creation of the protectorate allowed them to block the advance of the Germans. British authority also prevented the Afrikaners from claiming more land.

The Bechuanaland Protectorate

In theory, the government of the Bechuanaland Protectorate was in the hands of Batswana royal families. In practice, however, the British interfered in Batswana affairs and set up their own governmental structure. The major function of this mixed local-colonial administration was to collect enough taxes to make the protectorate self-supporting, so that Great Britain didn't have to spend money running it. The Batswana kings protested when boundaries were drawn through their traditional lands and often disagreed about where the new borders were placed. The kings were afraid that British laws might jeopardize the customary income from the payment of tribute.

Africans were also concerned about the activities of a trading firm called the British South Africa Company (BSAC). A wealthy politician named Cecil Rhodes ran the BSAC. In the 1890s, Rhodes tried to gain control of Bechuanaland. He wanted to connect by rail his holdings in the Cape Colony (modern-day Cape Province, South Africa) to his new lands in present-day Zimbabwe. To avoid conflicts with local leaders about land rights and to build the railroad quickly, Rhodes asked the British to give him control of the protectorate. He argued that the railroad could strengthen Great Britain's presence in Africa by connecting the Cape Colony with lands far to the north. In 1894 it seemed clear that the British would give Bechuanaland to Rhodes's company. But the next year, kings Khama III (of the Bangwato), Bathoen (of the Bangwaketse), and Sebele (of the Bakwena) traveled to Great Britain to protest the proposed transfer. They gained the support of Christian groups and British organizations that wanted to preserve African land rights. Because of the kings' efforts, the British government did not award Bechuanaland to Rhodes. Instead, the British gave the BSAC three narrow sections of land in eastern Bechuanaland. They told Rhodes that he could build his railway in this territory.

From left: **Kings Sebele, Bathoen, and Khama III** meet with a British pastor in London to protest the transfer of their land to Cecil Rhodes.

South African Pressures

In 1910 Afrikaner politicians established the self-governing Union of South Africa. It absorbed British Bechuanaland that same year. Leaders of the independent Afrikaner state also wanted the Bechuanaland Protectorate to be under their control. But once again, the kings of several Batswana groups petitioned for Bechuanaland to remain under British authority. They knew that South Africa was passing harsh laws that limited or denied the rights of Africans. The kings did not want these same laws to govern them.

Afrikaner politicians asked British authorities many times to release the protectorate to them. But the territory still remained under British control. Nevertheless, the colonial administration did little to establish industries, roads, schools, or health services within the colony. In fact, the protectorate's British high commissioner himself was not even in Bechuanaland. His headquarters were in Mafikeng, a city in South Africa.

The failure to develop trade, industries, and social services limited job opportunities in the colony. Many Africans in Bechuanaland were forced to work outside the protectorate. Some became migrant laborers in South Africa, where they worked for very low wages. To some extent, the colonial government regarded Bechuanaland's population as a cheap labor pool and neglected the future of the colony.

World Wars

Soon after the formation of the Union of South Africa in 1910, World War I (1914–1918) broke out. The protectorate's soldiers fought with the British against Germany. But beyond this involvement, the conflict had little direct impact on the protectorate.

Germany lost the war. As a result of postwar peace conferences, the German colony of South-West Africa came under South Africa's control. Thereafter, white-ruled governments surrounded Bechuanaland.

Despite these international changes, the protectorate had gradually begun to develop. In 1919 the British formed the Native Advisory Council (later called the African Council). The council advised the British high commissioner on African concerns.

The council's representatives were the kings of major Batswana groups and their chosen associates. At first, these leaders came only from the southern kingdoms. In 1931, however, the Batswana joined. In 1940 the Bangwato sent their first delegates. Among the Bangwato representatives was Tshekedi Khama. He was the guardian and uncle of the young, uncrowned kgosi Seretse Khama, who was the grandson of Khama III.

At its meetings, the African Council continued to oppose union with South Africa. By the start of World War II (1939–1945), about half of the protectorate's African males between fifteen and forty-four years old were working in South Africa. The council's members worried about South Africa's increasingly harsh laws of apartheid. These rules segregated black Africans and white Africans in South Africa and discriminated against blacks. Apartheid laws included restrictions on housing, landownership, and political rights for black South Africans.

Apartheid is the Afrikaner word for "apartness."

During the war, the council supported Great Britain. About ten thousand Batswana soldiers fought in the Middle East and Italy. After training in the city of Lobatse, the troops formed antiaircraft regiments and gun crews. Members of royal Batswana families participated in military expeditions to help Britain win the war.

In World War II's aftermath, Bechuanaland's colonial authorities faced a changed population. Bechuanaland became home to an entire generation of Africans who were neither herders, farmers, nor traditional leaders. These manual laborers hated apartheid. This view united African workers and the Batswana elite, who had long resisted becoming part of South Africa. As a result, both sections of Bechuanaland society began to support the idea of self-rule for the protectorate.

Troops from Bechuanaland help Italian civilians repair a railroad bridge destroyed by retreating German troops during World War II.

Seretse Khama and Independence

In the mid-1900s, a new event further stirred the fires of independence. That occasion was the royal marriage of the Bangwato kgosi, Seretse Khama. In 1948, while studying in Britain, Seretse Khama married a white Englishwoman named Ruth Williams. He returned to Bechuanaland with his new wife in 1949 to take over the kingship. But his uncle Tshekedi Khama and other members of the traditional elite opposed his mixed marriage. So did the white-ruled governments of Southern Rhodesia (modern-day Zimbabwe) and South Africa. To the colonial authorities, the tension seemed serious enough to justify keeping Tshekedi and Seretse apart. The British were also trying to please the pro-apartheid regimes in South Africa and Southern Rhodesia. Great Britain had strong economic ties with these governments.

In 1950, supposedly in an effort to ease tensions, British leaders invited Seretse Khama to visit Great Britain. But these same authorities then refused to allow him to return to Bechuanaland unless he gave up the kingship. The stated reason for this refusal was the rift between the king and his uncle. But even after the two men resolved their differences in 1952, Britain continued to restrict Seretse's freedom. These actions were based on the British government's desire not to upset white-ruled South Africa.

Seretse Khama and his wife, Ruth Williams, walk through a crowd of supporters in Bechuanaland.

Tshekedi Khama

For the next several years, many Bangwato people in Bechuanaland protested Seretse's treatment. They refused to cooperate with the colonial government. But Seretse strongly desired to serve his country. So in 1956, he agreed not to accept the Bangwato kingship, and the British allowed him to go back to Bechuanaland. When Seretse Khama returned to the protectorate soon afterward, he became a leader in the movement for self-rule.

Political Parties Form

In addition to Seretse Khama, other African politicians were also active at this time. Philip Matante, Motsamai Mpho, and K. T. Motsete were all prominent leaders. In 1960 they formed the Bechuanaland Peoples' Party (later the Botswana Peoples' Party, or BPP). The BPP called for rapid social and political reform, a pro-African constitution, and the expulsion of white settlers.

Meanwhile, Seretse Khama and others formed the Bechuanaland (later Botswana) Democratic Party (BDP). Although the Bangwato dominated Seretse Khama's party, the BDP gained widespread support.

In 1963 the British announced that they had a timetable for Bechuanaland's independence. At that time, Great Britain's empire around the world was beginning to crumble. Many of its colonies were winning their independence. The first step was to set up an election process. Bechuanaland's Africans registered to vote in 1964, and the territory's first elections took place in 1965. Seretse Khama and the BDP—helped by the leader's power base and national reputation—won 80 percent of the votes.

That same year, Seretse Khama became prime minister. He oversaw the peaceful transition of governmental authority from the Bechuanaland Protectorate to the Republic of Botswana. The republic was established on September 30, 1966. At that time, Seretse Khama became its first president.

In 1966 Britain's Queen Elizabeth II knighted Seretse Khama, making him Sir Seretse Khama. Knighting is a symbolic honor given to a person for service to Great Britain.

The Republic's Early Years

Following independence, Seretse Khama faced Botswana's lack of economic development. The colonial government had not built strong transportation or communications systems or started many industries.

The new nation also lacked access to the sea, except through white-ruled South Africa, South-West Africa, and Mozambique. Botswana needed goods, markets, and communication systems from those states to survive.

Despite this dependence, the new nation spoke out against South Africa and Southern Rhodesia's apartheid policies. Botswana publicly supported black Africans' struggles for reform and liberation in these countries—but continued to trade with them. Meanwhile, the president improved relations with Great Britain. He also established links with other self-ruled nations in Africa. Many of them had also recently won independence from European rule. In these ways, Seretse Khama hoped to obtain funds for development projects within Botswana. He also wanted to reduce the dominance of the Batswana ruling class, particularly regarding cattle ownership and land rights.

No matter how much the Botswana government tried, however, it could not remain completely apart from tensions in neighboring states. Southern Rhodesia, for example, experienced a civil war between 1972 and 1979. Thousands of civilians fled to Botswana for safety. So did guerrilla fighters (forces who launch surprise attacks or practice unconventional warfare). On several occasions, Rhodesian bombers attacked refugee camps in Botswana. After Rhodesia became independent as Zimbabwe in 1980, the refugees returned to their homeland.

Another group of people also entered the country in the 1970s, as Botswana received exiles from white-ruled South Africa. Hostility sometimes erupted between the two countries. South African officials accused Botswana of protecting revolutionary groups that sought to topple South Africa's pro-apartheid government. One such group was the African National Congress, which at the time was outlawed. Although Botswana denied this charge, South African planes attacked across the border. The raid killed Botswanans as well as South Africans.

Despite these international issues, Seretse Khama stabilized Botswana. A small but vocal political opposition to his government led to open discussions of important issues. In three elections—in 1969, 1974, and 1979—more than one party campaigned for seats in the legislature. In each election, however, the BDP maintained its majority in the National Assembly.

In addition, the nation's economic footing was strong, thanks to diamond mining. This industry took off in the 1970s and soon brought significant income to Botswana.

◑ New Leaders

In 1980 President Seretse Khama died of cancer. His vice president, Quett Masire, succeeded him in office. Masire was officially elected

In 1984 **Quett Masire** was officially elected president after serving in the office following the death of Seretse Khama.

president in 1984 and again in 1989. The BDP continued to dominate the legislature.

President Masire's administration faced the difficult task of managing Botswana's economic growth. Another challenge was new relations with a postapartheid South Africa. Apartheid practices had largely ended by 1993. That same year, international trading sanctions (restrictions) against South Africa were lifted. This change brought more competition for foreign investment in the region.

The Masire government also began exploring trade connections through the Southern African Development Community (SADC). This group was made up of nine countries that relied economically on South Africa. The SADC has provided a framework for regional cooperation to spur economic growth, foster trade, and achieve financial independence.

One of the SADC's early goals was the construction of a highway connecting the opposite coasts of southern Africa. The project was spurred, in part, by the independence of Namibia in 1990. Work began in the early 1990s, and the highway opened in 1998. It connected Namibia's Walvis Bay to the port of Maputo, Mozambique. Its path across Botswana (and also South Africa) gave the nation new and easier access to the sea. In addition, the direct lane of transportation decreased Botswana's need to send most of its cargo through South Africa.

The diamond business was still booming too. In the mid-1990s, Botswana was the world's leading producer of gem-quality diamonds and received 80 percent of its export earnings from diamond sales. The government funneled much of this money into strengthening rural development projects and into creating jobs. South African firms owned significant shares in Botswana's mining industry, however, and the gems often had to travel to overseas markets through South Africa. Botswanan leaders and economists worried about relying so heavily on their southern neighbor.

In 1998 President Masire retired. His vice president, Festus Mogae, became the new president. About this same time, different opinions arose among members of one of Botswana's opposition parties, the Botswana National Front (BNF). As a result, some members of the BNF formed a new political party, called the Botswana Congress Party (BCP). The BCP soon became an influential group. Nevertheless, the BDP continued to dominate Botswana's government. Voters officially elected Mogae as president in 1999.

Ethnic Tensions and Ongoing Developments

Amid these political developments, another issue took the forefront. The government had been working for several years to relocate Botswana's San people. The San's traditional homelands include an area that had become part of the Central Kalahari Game Reserve. The huge reserve covers more than 20,000 square miles (51,800 sq.

Festus Mogae

km). But Botswana officials argued that San settlements in the reserve were beyond the reach of the country's infrastructure (basic systems such as energy, transportation, and communications). They also said that having people in the reserve hurt the wildlife there. They called for the San to move to relocation camps outside the reserve. The government promised to provide resources such as schools and other facilities in these new settlements.

Hundreds of San did move. But some refused to leave their homes. By the early 2000s, the issue had attracted broader attention. The government insisted relocation was voluntary. However, spokespeople and activist groups for the San said that the government had cut off water and food supplies to the San who remained on the land. They also said that government workers threatened and harassed San families. And they claimed that the government's main motive was a desire to exploit the area's potential diamond reserves. Botswana officials denied these accusations. But human rights concerns remained.

In 2003 a San group began a court case against the government, asking for the right to remain in the reserve. The lawsuit hit a snag in 2005 when the government changed the nation's constitution by lessening protections for Botswana's ethnic minorities. Nevertheless, the court ruled in favor of the San in late 2006. In the following months, some San families began returning to their lands within the reserve. But they still faced challenges. The government imposed strict limits on hunting in the reserve, as well as on the use of boreholes to provide water.

In early 2008, President Festus Mogae retired at the end of his second term in office. (He had been reelected in 2004.) Mogae's vice president was Ian Khama—the son of Botswana's first president, Seretse Khama. In April 2008, the younger Khama was inaugurated as the nation's new leader.

A HISTORIC VICTORY

The San lawsuit against Botswana's government was the longest-running and most expensive court case in the nation's history. The judge who ruled in favor of the San called the government's actions "unlawful and unconstitutional."

In April 2008, Ian Khama *(right)* becomes the fourth president of Botswana.

 Visit www.vgsbooks.com for links to websites with up-to-date news stories about Botswana, and find out more about the government of Botswana and its leaders.

▶ Government

Botswana's executive power rests in a president. This president is chosen by the National Assembly. The chief executive's powers include calling and dissolving the assembly and approving all taxation bills. A cabinet (group of advisers) assists the president. Most cabinet members come from the assembly.

The National Assembly is the larger and more powerful body in Botswana's legislative branch, or parliament. It consists of fifty-seven directly elected members. The president and the assembly itself choose another four delegates. Like the president, assembly members serve five-year terms. Citizens who are eighteen years of age and older can vote, and they choose assembly members by secret ballot.

The other part of the legislative branch is the thirty-five-member House of Chiefs. Traditional tribal leaders elect thirty of these chiefs. The other five are appointed by the president. Eight of these chiefs are traditional leaders of Botswana's eight principal Batswana groups. Members serve five-year terms. Also called the Ntlo ya Dikgosi, the House of Chiefs advises the parliament, especially on matters affecting Botswana's ethnic minorities. Traditional Batswana leaders also serve on district councils and land boards. They play minor judicial roles and continue to hold public meetings.

The National Assembly building in Gaborone

Botswana's 1965 constitution contains a code of human rights. The nation's courts help uphold this code. The judicial system consists of customary (traditional) and civil courts. Batswana leaders preside over customary courts and exercise some power, such as in cases of cattle theft. Civil courts include regional courts and courts of appeal. The High Court is located in Lobatse.

For administrative purposes, Botswana is divided into nine district councils and four town councils. Each has an elected governing body and an executive commissioner. The councils finance primary education, supply licenses to local businesses, and collect taxes. They also help to plan development projects and to budget funds.

THE PEOPLE

About 1.8 million people live in Botswana. The nation's average population density is low, at only 3 people per square mile (1.2 per sq. km). By comparison, an average of 40 residents live in each square mile (15 per sq. km) of Botswana's neighbor South Africa. The average density across all of southern Africa is 21 people per square mile (8.1 per sq. km).

The population of Botswana is distributed very unevenly. The highest concentrations of people occur along a north-south corridor in the eastern portion of the country. In this area, the water supply is more reliable, farmable land is available, and better health care and education facilities exist. This high-population region also has access to the nation's main railway line.

Partly due to a low average life expectancy of 49 years, much of Botswana's population is very young. Almost 40 percent of all Botswanans are under the age of 15. Only 3 percent of the population is over the age of 65.

Ethnic and Language Groups

Botswana contains one large ethnic group and several smaller ethnic groups. Many of these communities share cultural traits and languages. The Batswana make up 95 percent of the African population in Botswana. They have a common history, language, and social organization. The Batswana are also closely related by language and cultural to Basotho peoples who live in Lesotho (a small country surrounded by South Africa) and South Africa. Eight main subgroups exist within the Batswana ethnicity.

The Batswana have long dominated Botswana's other ethnic groups and continue to be most influential in the government. All the country's presidents have come from the Batswana. Seretse Khama was a member of the Bangwato royal family, as is his son Ian Khama. Festus Mogae is also Bangwato, while Quett Masire belongs to the Bangwaketse subgroup.

In traditional Batswana society, an upper middle class rules over the majority of the people. This pattern continues in Botswana. Even Batswana subgroups are ranked by seniority. The oldest—the Bakwena—is usually at the top of the list. The Bangwato, the Bangwaketse, and the Batwana generally follow the Bakwena in rank. The other main subgroups are the Bakgatla, the Balete, the Barolong, and the Batlokwa. Members of all these clans speak Setswana—the Bantu language of the Batswana. Along with English, Setswana is the nation's official language. Some people in South Africa, Namibia, and Zimbabwe also speak Setswana.

While much smaller in number than the Batswana, the San people are a historically important group in Botswana. Their ancestors were the original inhabitants of the area. An estimated fifty thousand to sixty thousand San live in modern Botswana, making up about 3 percent of the nation's total population. The San are of small physical stature. They traditionally speak with a click language, so called because the action of the tongue against the roof of the mouth produces a clicking sound. In Botswana most San use the Nharo click language. Only about three thousand or fewer San continue to live in traditional ways in the Kalahari Desert. They continue to hunt animals and gather food. These San communities follow a mostly nomadic lifestyle. They move frequently to follow game or find water. But most members of the group work on farms or in cities. Many have adopted the Batswana culture that dominates the country.

Botswana's other minorities include the Bakalanga and the Bayei. Together they account for approximately 1 percent of the nation's population. In Botswana's past, the Batswana conquered these groups and made them into a labor force for Batswanan needs. As a result, tension remains between these groups and the still-dominant Batswana.

The remaining 1 percent of Botswana's population includes communities of black South Africans and Zimbabweans. They have arrived in Botswana since the 1970s, when strife disrupted their homelands. Many Zimbabweans continue to arrive.

Botswana is also home to Europeans and white South Africans. Compared to the overall population, a disproportionate number of these white citizens occupy important technical and policy-making positions in national organizations and businesses. In part by providing proper training, the Botswana government seeks to bring more black Botswanans into these fields.

◉ Daily Life

Descendants of cattle herders and farmers, many modern-day Botswanans still live at least partly off the land. But poor soil and lack of rainfall prevent the majority of Botswanans from producing enough food to feed their families.

Most of Botswana's people live in towns or small villages in the country's eastern one-third. Many of these settlements still follow a traditional layout. They consist of a cluster of round, straw-roofed houses built of mud bricks. Some other homes are made of cement blocks with metal roofs.

Life in these Botswanan villages often follows a traditional pattern. A male-dominated council, usually led by the head of the oldest or largest family, decides which part of the village land each family group will farm. Agricultural output remains low, and few people can support themselves solely by farming or keeping cattle. As a result, men often

A traditional Botswanan home stands next to modern dwellings. The round mud-brick homes common in Botswana are called *rondavels*. The name comes from the Afrikaner language, Afrikaans.

leave their villages in search of temporary work. Botswanan women then carry the double burden of farming and raising a family. Women may hand over some of the daily care of their children to grandparents or young girls.

In Gaborone and other cities in Botswana, such traditional ways of life have changed over the years. For example, many people live in apartment buildings. Large cities often feature a modern, central downtown. And many women in cities work outside the home in professional careers.

But old ideas about gender roles remain. Botswanan women often face discrimination. Traditional laws limit their rights to own property, for instance. Many women suffer physical and sexual abuse at the hands of their husbands. Some new laws increase and protect women's rights. And women are gradually finding greater representation in the government—both modern and traditional. In 2003 a woman became the leader of the Balete people, marking the first time a woman led a Batswana group. But Botswanan women continue to face challenges.

Discrimination against some ethnic groups is also a problem in Botswana. The San, in particular, continue to face prejudice. They also have limited access to good education and jobs.

City residents have a different lifestyle than Botswanans who live in rural areas. City dwellers are more likely to drive and to work in offices and shops, for example.

⊙ Health

Before independence, the colonial government spent little money on developing medical facilities. Missionaries staffed and funded most health clinics. After 1966, however, Botswana began working to improve the health of its citizens.

The new projects made good progress in some areas. National campaigns began to vaccinate babies against major diseases such as polio, measles, and diphtheria. In modern Botswana, 80 to 90 percent of children receive the most important vaccinations. In addition, clinics and other health-care facilities exist around the country. But the nation has only about 4 doctors for every 10,000 people. And poor sanitation and substandard diets still endanger the health of many Botswanans, especially in rural areas.

Botswana's infant mortality rate is 44 deaths in every 1,000 live births. And out of every 10,000 live births, more than 30 mothers die each year due to complications during pregnancy or childbirth. The World Health Organization (WHO) estimates 124 deaths in every 1,000 children under the age of 5. (By comparison, about 69 children per every 1,000 die under the age of 5 in South Africa. In Britain the figure is 6 deaths per 1,000 children under 5.) Poor nutrition is one of the major causes of such deaths.

Visit www.vgsbooks.com for links to get more information about the daily life and health conditions of people in Botswana. Learn about what challenges Botswana is facing.

HIV/AIDS is by far the biggest factor in modern Botswana's health statistics. Botswana's first case of AIDS was reported in 1985. In the twenty-first century, the nation has the second-highest rate of HIV/AIDS in the world, after the southern African nation of Swaziland. More than 24 percent of people between the ages of 15 and 49 are infected. The spread of this disease has caused Botswanans' life expectancy to plummet. The average citizen born in the 1990s could expect to live into his or her mid-60s. In the twenty-first century, that figure had fallen to just 34 years.

Similarly, Botswana once had a high population growth rate compared to many other African countries, at 3.1 percent. But deaths due to HIV/AIDS have lowered the nation's growth rate to –0.1 percent. That means that the population is shrinking. WHO officials estimate that the disease causes eighteen thousand deaths yearly and that more than 110,000 Botswanan children have lost one or both parents to HIV/AIDS.

This poster advertises **an HIV counseling and testing center** in Gaborone.

> **"We are threatened with extinction. People are dying in chillingly high numbers. It is a crisis of the first magnitude."**
>
> —former president Festus Mogae, speaking in 2001 about HIV/AIDS

Botswana's government and international agencies run programs to fight the spread of HIV/AIDS. One focus of these efforts is educating Botswanans about the causes of the disease, which is spread by body fluids exchanged during sex or through blood, and how to prevent it. Awareness clubs in schools target youth, while billboards and other media are aimed at the general public. Health organizations provide medication and treatment to infected people—including those who cannot afford to pay for medical care.

But obstacles hinder the fight to slow the disease's spread. Traditional social values in Botswana prohibit talking openly about sex. Therefore, many people are unwilling to talk about the disease or to be tested for it. In addition, people who are already infected often feel too ashamed to seek treatment.

◉ Education

Children in cities across Botswana have long received more schooling than rural children. In the 1970s, the government spent funds to increase the number of primary schools in the countryside. But rural schools continue to lag behind urban facilities in teacher training, enrollment, and other areas.

Still, Botswana's educational system is above average for sub-Saharan Africa (south of the Sahara). The government spends about one-fifth of its budget on education. The country's overall literacy rate (the percentage of adults who can read and write) is more than 80 percent. And Botswanan children benefit from a high teacher-to-student ratio. For approximately every twenty-five elementary students, there is one teacher. In secondary schools, each teacher handles an average of about thirteen students. More than 90 percent of these teachers have training—though more urban teachers tend to have better training than those in rural areas.

While the law does not require Botswanan children to go to school, most of them do. UNESCO estimates that about 82 percent of all school-age Botswanans attend classes. Botswana also boasts a very high rate of female enrollment compared to many African nations. More students go to elementary school than to secondary school, however. The percentage of children enrolled in secondary classes drops to about 60 percent, with actual attendance rates even lower.

A fairly small number of students go on to colleges and universities. The University of Botswana, in Gaborone, opened in 1982. The school offers undergraduate degrees in many fields, including education, medicine, engineering, and business. More than fifteen thousand people attend the university. Students looking for higher education can also choose from many technical and vocational schools targeting specific areas of training. These institutions include the Botswana College of Agriculture, the Botswana Institute of Administration and Commerce, and others.

A teacher reads a story to children at a **community school.**

Cultural Life

Botswana's ethnic mixture and its colonial past give it a blend of customs and traditions. While the Batswana have been dominant throughout history, other influences have left their mark on the modern nation's cultural life.

▷ Religion

Like many parts of Botswanan culture, ancient ways and European ideas mix in the country's religion. Because of missionary activity in the nineteenth century, some of Botswana's people are practicing Christians. Some are Catholics, while others follow Protestant branches of Christianity.

Many Botswanans follow traditional faiths. These older beliefs often revolve around the powers and responsibilities of local rulers and healers. Spiritual meaning is attached to nature and to health. Believers regard individual actions as the causes of drought and sickness. They also have deep respect for their ancestors.

web enhanced @ www.vgsbooks.com

It is unclear how many Botswanans are Christians and how many follow traditional faiths, because so many mix and blend beliefs. For example, people who follow some Christian customs may also turn to traditional healers during sickness.

Very small numbers of Botswanans follow Islam, Judaism, or other religions. Many of these people live in urban areas. Others follow no religion.

The San people have their own set of religious ideas. They honor nature and respect a divine creator. Dance rituals are important to traditional San believers, and men sometimes go into a trance while dancing. The San consider this state a form of communication between humans and a supernatural power.

Holidays and Festivals

Botswana's Christians observe a number of religious holidays. Easter and Christmas are the most important of these celebrations.

Dancers in traditional dress perform at a ceremony celebrating forty years of independence from British colonial rule. The statues are of chiefs Khama III, Sebele, and Bathoen, who were instrumental in keeping Botswana separate from South Africa in the 1890s.

On Easter, families and friends gather for special meals. Many also attend church services. Christmas, too, brings loved ones together for worship, as well as holiday songs and gift exchanges. And among followers of all faiths, life events such as marriage and the birth of a child are causes for celebration.

Some holidays in Botswana are connected to political history. Sir Seretse Khama Day, for example, honors the nation's first president. It takes place on his birthday, July 1. Botswana Day, on September 30, celebrates the country's 1966 independence from Great Britain. Labor Day on May 1 and New Year's Day on January 1 are other secular (nonreligious) celebrations.

Botswanans also enjoy several annual arts festivals. Ever since 1987, the Maitisong Festival has taken place each year in Gaborone. Usually falling in March, April, or May, it is the nation's largest performing arts event. The nine-day festival brings together musicians, dancers, comics, and other artists from Botswana and beyond. Food vendors supply festivalgoers with snacks and beverages.

July brings the National Music Eisteddfod in Selebi-Phikwe. This event focuses on traditional music and dance. Groups from around the nation come to this centrally located town to perform. Some of the dances and songs are regional, while others belong to specific ethnic groups.

Arts and Crafts

Botswana is home to a variety of visual artists. They work in both fine arts and more traditional crafts. Within the fine arts world, Isaac Chibua is a rising star. This young painter and sculptor has won several awards, and his works have been displayed as far away as China. While many of his sculptures are abstract, he also often depicts people, including miners and musicians.

Some of the nation's artists represent ethnic minorities. Xhose Noxo, also known as Cgoise, is a San artist from northwestern Botswana. Her brightly colored paintings show native animals and plants and traditional activities, such as women preparing food. Another San painter is Gamnqoa Kukama. His works depict animals of the Kalahari Desert, as well as the hunting traditions of the San people.

The National Museum and Art Gallery in Gaborone opened in 1968. It displays paintings, sculpture, photographs, and other works of fine art. The museum also holds many examples of crafts. Traditional crafts are an important part of Botswana's artistic culture. These works continue to make up an important part of daily life. Local art councils and museums work to encourage the preservation and growth of these elements of national culture.

Basket weaving is one of the most famous and treasured crafts in the country. Botswanan women weave baskets using leaves from the *mokola* palm tree, which grows in the Okavango Delta. Weavers twist and coil these leaves to form patterned, multicolored baskets.

Two women weave baskets as part of a community income-generation project. Traditional crafts are one way for Botswanans to make money.

A man works on a **wood carving** in a village in the Okavango Delta.

Other regional crafts include pottery, leatherworking, and carvings of wood and bone. Some of Botswana's craft traditions began to die out during the colonial era. But following independence, many people worked to revive age-old arts. Many of these crafts gradually became sources of income in modern Botswana. For example, hand-woven rugs and wall hangings from Oodi (near Gaborone) and Serowe are part of a growing export industry. Some women have formed groups to sell their baskets to buyers all over the world. Tourists visiting Botswana also buy these beautiful local crafts.

AN EYE FOR THE ARTS

In 1968 an organization called the Botswana Society formed to support the nation's arts. In present-day Botswana, this group continues to encourage literary work in the social sciences, arts, and humanities. It publishes *Botswana Notes and Records*, containing articles about life in Botswana.

◎ Literature

Botswana's earliest literary tradition was oral. Storytellers shared historical events, religious lessons, and folktales, passing these stories down through generations. Printed literature was not widely available until the 1800s. And even then, most of it was religious in nature. Christian missionaries translated the Bible into the Setswana language, for instance.

As time went on—and especially after independence—Botswanan authors began writing more of their own works. Many published in Setswana, but some wrote in English. Leetile Disang Raditladi (1910–1971) was a politician who also became a prominent Batswana author. Writing in Setswana, he published award-winning plays and poetry. He also worked as a journalist.

M. O. M. Seboni also wrote in Setswana and worked to preserve Batswana heritage through his publications. Seboni began his literary career in the 1960s with a children's novel entitled *Rammone of the Kalahari*. He also wrote traditional poems and translated Shakespeare's plays *The Merchant of Venice* and *Henry IV* into Setswana.

Andrew Sesinyi's book *Love on the Rocks* was published in 1983. This romantic novel for teenagers quickly became a big hit in Botswana and beyond. Sesinyi continues to write novels and is also venturing into nonfiction work based on his own life.

Novelist Unity Dow is another important author in modern Botswana. Her books include *Far and Beyon'*, *The Screaming of the Innocent*, and *Juggling Truths*. Her main characters are usually women, and her works frequently address Botswanan issues such as AIDS, poverty, and domestic abuse. Dow is also a lawyer, judge, and human rights activist.

Other contemporary authors include the poet Barolong Seboni—M. O. M. Seboni's nephew. In addition to his own poetry and his work as a professor, Barolong Seboni has worked on a project that his uncle began. He has translated his uncle's compilation of 1,400 Botswana proverbs from Setswana into English.

Moteane Melamu has published a collection of short stories titled *Living and Partly Living*, as well as the novel *Children of the Twilight*. He is a professor at the University of Botswana.

TELLING STORIES

"My name is Monei Ntuka and this is the story of my childhood in the village of Mochudi, in the then British Bechuanaland Protectorate, in the mid to late sixties. It is, of course, not the whole story of my youth, for didn't my grandmother Mma-Tsietsi, mother of my father, tell me many times, 'A tongue can talk until numb with fatigue, but it can never tell the whole story'? And didn't she gently admonish me, when I would go on and on, saying, 'Child of my child, a good story teller knows when to stop, just as a dreamer knows when to wake up.'"

—Unity Dow,
Juggling Truths (2003)

Music and Dance

Botswana's people enjoy a mixture of modern and traditional musical styles. Historically, different regions and ethnic groups within Botswana have each had their own styles of music and dance. Some of these traditional genres are in danger of disappearing. But efforts to preserve the nation's cultural heritage have slowed their decline. For instance, the Mogwana Dance Troupe, based in Gaborone, formed in 1991 to keep Botswana's ethnic dance and music alive. And the Kuru San Traditional Dance Festival takes place each August in the Kalahari village of D'kar. This event highlights dances of the San people. Many San dances are tied to specific activities and events such as hunting outings, weddings, or the birth of a child. The festival also features traditional San music.

> San music features a twangy instrument known as the thumb piano. This miniature piano has tiny metal keys. Players use their thumbs to hit the keys and create musical notes.

Individual musicians have also specialized in traditional forms. One was Ratsie Setlhako, who played the *segaba*. This indigenous (native) instrument has only one string, but skilled players can produce many notes. Similarly, singer George Swabi and guitarist Andries Bok have worked to keep folk music alive.

Young Botswanans also enjoy a variety of modern popular music. In the past, much of it came from outside the country. But more and

The Mogwana Dance Troupe performs in 2004.

more local artists are gaining recognition. Hip-hop artists include the Wizards, Ignition, and 3rd Mind. Rock and heavy metal bands such as Nodd, Skinflint, and Wrust are also based in Botswana.

Much Botswanan music blends influences from various sources. For example, *gumba gumba* combines elements of jazz and traditional African music. *Kwasa kwasa* is a regional variation on African rumba beats. Many listeners enjoy dancing to this music in nightclubs. *Kwaito*, a modern, beat-heavy genre that developed in South Africa in the 1990s, is also popular. Kwaito artists may rap or sing, and lyrics often address political themes. Singer Lesego Bile is one of the first female kwaito artists. And the Botswanan musician Odirile Sento, also known as Vee, has created his own blend of kwaito and kwasa kwasa, called *kwasa kwaito*.

 Visit www.vgsbooks.com for links to websites with additional information about the culture of Botswana. Listen to traditional Botswanan music, and learn more about its literature.

Sports and Entertainment

Sports are an important part of Botswana's social life. Soccer—which Botswanans call football—is the most popular team activity and spectator sport. The national team—nicknamed the Zebras—

Bokhutlo Gabriel *(left)* of the **Zebras** goes after the ball against a Chinese player during a pre-Olympic tournament in 2007.

Soccer is the most popular sport in Botswana among people of all ages. In this village in northern Botswana, children pass the time with a casual game.

competes against other African teams. The Zebras home field is the Botswana National Stadium in Gaborone. This venue holds more than twenty thousand spectators. Soccer matches between villages also draw many fans.

Cricket is also popular. This complicated game arrived in Africa with British colonists. It involves batters who attempt to score runs against the opposite team. Botswana has a national squad that, like the soccer team, plays in regional matches.

Athletic clubs exist in the nation's urban areas, but they are used mostly by the wealthy. Gambling casinos in Gaborone and other cities attract many tourists from South Africa. An eighteen-hole golf course is located in the capital,

THE SPORTING LIFE

Botswana took part in the Olympic Games for the first time in 1980. The nation sent seven track-and-field athletes to the Summer Olympics in Moscow, Russia (then part of the USSR, or Soviet Union, a union of fifteen republics). Botswanan athletes have taken part in every Summer Olympics since 1980 but have never gone to the Winter Olympics.

and swimming pools exist in major towns. A small yacht club is situated at the Gaborone Dam, where sailing and windsurfing are favorite activities. Horseback riding is also popular, while other Botswanans like to play tennis and softball.

For most Botswanans, conversation and storytelling remain common forms of recreation. Dance halls, bars, and movie theaters exist in most towns and are very popular meeting places for people at all levels of society.

Many Botswanans also turn to radio and television for entertainment. Radio Botswana, a state-run station, plays music, as well as news and educational programs in both English and Setswana. Several private stations also broadcast in the country. Similarly, the government operates Botswana Television (BTV), while a private channel based in Gaborone shows additional programming.

Filmmaking in Botswana has long focused on wildlife and nature specials. But in 2007, the television movie *The No. 1 Ladies' Detective Agency* was filmed in Botswana. While the director and writers were not Botswanan, the large-scale production gave local film buffs the welcome chance to work on a major project. Still, moviemaking in the country has yet to take off.

Anthony Minghella, the director of **The No. 1 Ladies' Detective Agency** *(center, in cap)*, gives advice to the cast before shooting a scene in 2007. Many Botswanans hope the movie will bring other projects to Botswana.

◉ Food

The relatively fertile lands in the east and in the inland delta of the Okavango provide most of Botswana's food. Three crops—millet, corn, and cassava (a starchy root)—form the basis of the national diet.

Farmers have cultivated millet and corn in Botswana for centuries. Millet is a tall, strong plant with a large head of grain. After farmers harvest millet, they pound it into flour with a large wooden pole. Cooks then make the flour into a porridge called *bogobe*. Similarly, most corn is mashed into another form of porridge that is a staple of the Botswanan diet.

Cassavas are large, long roots that resemble hard potatoes. Botswanans eat raw cassavas in the fields, bake them in the embers of

VEGETABLE STEW

This tasty and hearty dish can be made with a wide variety of vegetables, depending on what's in season or available. Botswanan cooks would serve a stew such as this with a porridge made from corn.

1 tablespoon canola or vegetable oil

1 medium onion, chopped

½ teaspoon turmeric

½ teaspoon paprika

1 teaspoon ground cumin

2 cloves garlic, minced

1 tablespoon freshly peeled and grated gingerroot

3 teaspoons tomato paste

1 large sweet potato, peeled and chopped

1 carrot, peeled and chopped

½ red bell pepper, cored, seeded, and chopped

½ cup fresh or frozen green beans, ends trimmed

2 cups vegetable stock

1. In a Dutch oven or large kettle, warm oil over medium heat. Add onion and sauté for about 5 minutes, or until soft and translucent.
2. Add turmeric, paprika, cumin, garlic, gingerroot, and tomato paste. Mix well and cook for 1 minute.
3. Add sweet potato, carrot, red bell pepper, and green beans. Stir well to coat vegetables with spices.
4. Add stock and bring to a boil over high heat. Reduce heat and simmer, partially covered, for about 30 minutes, or until tender. Serve hot.

Serves 4

small fires, or soak and grate them into a coarse flour. Cassava flour has little nutritional value, although it can be stored for weeks and is relatively easy to transport. Cooks often season the flour with spices and seeds.

Most Botswanans regularly eat a combination of millet, sorghum (a grain), and corn. Goat, beef, and chicken are popular meats and often are featured in stews. For special occasions, families often enjoy a simple, slow-cooked meat dish called *seswaa* (also known as *chotlho*). Gourds and beans also help to round out meals, as well as some vegetables, including cabbage and spinach. For dessert, diners may enjoy fruits such as berries, melon, mangoes, or papayas. Tea is often served with meals, sometimes sweetened with sugar. *Bojalwa*, a locally brewed beer made from grains, is a popular adult beverage.

Diet varies between rural and urban Botswanans and depending on income. For example, wealthier people generally have greater access to meat, eggs, and fresh fruits and vegetables. A growing number of people—especially in cities—eat processed foods, fast food, or foreign dishes such as Chinese, Indian, and Europeanized food.

A family enjoys a melon for dessert. Fresh fruit is a common way to end a Botswanan meal.

THE ECONOMY

Botswana is something of an economic puzzle. On the one hand, the country contains many valuable minerals, such as diamonds, copper, nickel, and coal. These deposits bring significant income to the nation. In addition, the country's inflation (the rate at which prices increase) is relatively low. And the average yearly income per person is more than twelve thousand dollars. (This figure uses purchasing power parity, or PPP. PPP is a value in "international dollars" that indicates how many goods and services money can buy in a given country.) This average income is high compared to most of Africa.

On the other hand, most Botswanans are poor. The country's wealth is not spread evenly among its people. A small section of the society—drawn from the traditional Batswana ruling class—is quite wealthy. Meanwhile, many other citizens struggle to make ends meet. And unemployment rates are high. Botswana's officials work to close this gap between the nation's rich and poor.

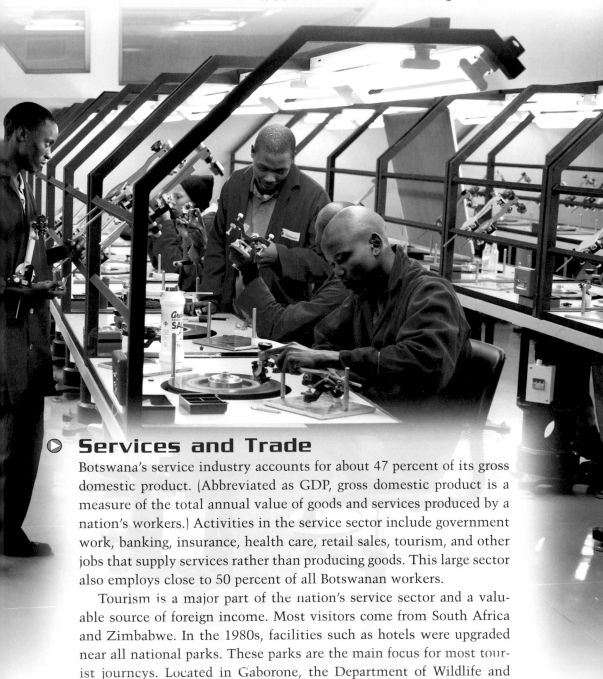

Services and Trade

Botswana's service industry accounts for about 47 percent of its gross domestic product. (Abbreviated as GDP, gross domestic product is a measure of the total annual value of goods and services produced by a nation's workers.) Activities in the service sector include government work, banking, insurance, health care, retail sales, tourism, and other jobs that supply services rather than producing goods. This large sector also employs close to 50 percent of all Botswanan workers.

Tourism is a major part of the nation's service sector and a valuable source of foreign income. Most visitors come from South Africa and Zimbabwe. In the 1980s, facilities such as hotels were upgraded near all national parks. These parks are the main focus for most tourist journeys. Located in Gaborone, the Department of Wildlife and National Parks runs a network of protected game sanctuaries.

Seasonal rains draw wildlife to the Chobe River between April and November. As a result, these months are the busiest season for

Chobe National Park. A series of roads takes vacationers through areas where giraffes, elephants, and rare white rhinoceroses can be viewed. The Moremi Wildlife Reserve, located on the edge of the Okavango Delta, is also very popular. In this rugged park, visitors usually need four-wheel-drive vehicles to see the region's large herds of zebras, wildebeests, kudu, and eland (antelope). Dozens of bird species also frequent the reserve.

Foreign trade is another important aspect of Botswana's economy. But the landlocked country lacks its own seaport. Relatively few good roads exist, and only one main railway crosses the country. As a result, sending goods to overseas markets is still difficult.

In part to ease such challenges, Botswana belongs to a trade organization called the Southern African Customs Union (SACU). The British created the SACU in 1910. It links the economies of Botswana, Lesotho, Namibia, South Africa, and Swaziland. The group's main goal is to ensure free trade among these five nations. Officials from each country meet annually to discuss important trade matters.

Botswana's leaders have also explored other trade connections in southern Africa, notably the Southern African Development Coordination Conference (SADCC). With its main office in Gaborone, the SADCC works to broaden Botswana's commercial contacts. In addition, the government has sought ties with African nations to the north, with Arab countries, and with European nations.

Most of Botswana's overall trading activity is with the SACU and its members. But the nation exports more goods to Britain than to any other single trading partner. Botswanan products also go to Zimbabwe, the United States, and various African and European destinations. The country imports goods from the same nations.

◉ Mining

Beginning in the 1970s, mining transformed Botswana's economy. The rapid expansion of local mining activities generated jobs and considerable foreign income. The mining industry employs only about 3 percent of the nation's workers. But it contributes more than 40 percent of the country's GDP.

In present-day Botswana, diamonds account for between 70 and 80 percent of the country's total export earnings. The nation remains among the largest diamond producers in the world. South Africa's De Beers Company and the Botswana government jointly own the nation's diamond

The Jwaneng diamond mine, about 80 miles (129 km) west of Gaborone, is one of Botswana's largest. Its name means "place of small stones" in Setswana.

Above: The largest diamond mine in the world is at Orapa, Botswana. *Inset:* A worker sorts raw diamonds at a factory in Gaborone.

mines. Pits at Orapa, Jwaneng, and Letlhakane contain substantial deposits. More than 30 million carats (the unit of weight for precious stones) of gem-quality diamonds are produced each year. Botswana's diamond industry directly employs thousands of people, and many more jobs result from the need for support services.

The Selebi-Phikwe nickel and copper mines are a major employer. Botswana annually produces about 40,000 tons (36,287 metric tons) of copper and nickel. But low world prices for these metals have posed a challenge for the mines and their workers.

Vast reserves of coal lie in eastern Botswana. Mining began in 1972. In the 2000s, miners extracted as much as 800,000 to 900,000 tons (725,748 to 816,466 metric tons) each year. The only major coal mine in the nation is the Morupule Coal Mine, located about 175 miles (282 km) northeast of Gaborone.

While the mining industry brings high earnings, it has also caused some problems. For example, some of the polluted waste from mine operations flows into the nation's rivers. This pollution endangers Botswana's limited water supply.

Manufacturing and Industry

Although manufacturing has expanded considerably since 1980, it still makes up only about 10 percent of the nation's GDP. The sector employs approximately 8 percent of the country's workers. A small domestic market and the easy availability of South African goods hamper the growth of Botswana's industrial sector. A shortage of skilled laborers has also hindered industrialization in Botswana.

Meat processing is one of the country's most valuable manufacturing activities. The Botswana Meat Commission (BMC) has facilities in Lobatse that are among the largest processing plants in Africa. The Lobatse plants can slaughter hundreds of cattle daily. A smaller slaughterhouse is located at Maun. Canning meat and preparing livestock by-products, such as hides and skins, are other activities of the cattle industry. A growing industry exists to cut and polish diamonds, though Botswana still exports many of its gems in their unfinished state.

Other manufacturing plants in Botswana tend to be small, and many are at least partially owned by foreigners. Few businesses exist in rural areas. Even most of the factories in larger towns employ relatively few people. Some of these firms weave cloth, make clothing, and assemble furniture.

Agriculture and Livestock

Although mining and manufacturing earn greater income, herding and farming employ far more Botswanans. About 39 percent of the country's people raise livestock or farm the land. But only about 3 percent of the nation's GDP comes from the combined activities of farming, hunting, fishing, and forestry.

Botswana's soil is more suited to producing pasture than crops. As a result, livestock dominates the agricultural sector. Cattle raising is a traditional occupation that is still important in modern Botswana. The number of cattle tripled in the decade after independence. While droughts and overgrazing have since reduced herds considerably, there are still more than twice as many cattle than humans in the nation.

CATTLE CUSTOMS

Historically, only members of royal or very wealthy Batswana families could own cattle. Most of the nation's herds are still owned by a small number of the people. These farmers may bring their cattle to slaughterhouses in Lobatse and Maun. The rest of the nation's livestock feed on the grazing lands of low-income herders. Few of these small-scale herders employ modern breeding methods and have efficient veterinary care.

Botswana is one of the main livestock producers in southern Africa, and beef is a major export.

Goats and sheep roam freely in most of Botswana. Drought and disease have affected these herds, but close to two million goats still graze, along with about three hundred thousand sheep. Farmers also raise chickens, turkeys, and ducks throughout the country.

In general, Botswana's soil is not very fertile. Less than 1 percent of the country's land is considered arable, or well suited to growing crops. Even in these areas, precipitation levels vary and water evaporates quickly. Thus, plants lose water so rapidly that crops sometimes fail even in years of normal rainfall. During the 1980s, the country faced a persistent drought. Despite the availability of underground water supplies, lack of rain cut the production of crops and livestock, particularly by small-scale farmers.

Major crops include corn, millet, sorghum, and several varieties of fruits and vegetables. But farmers cannot produce enough of these foods to meet the country's own needs. As a result, Botswana imports large amounts of food. Much of it comes from South Africa. But government programs have tried to broaden Botswana's agricultural output. Farmers have begun planting more cash-earning crops, such as peanuts, cotton, and sunflowers.

A man herds his flock of goats in the Kalahari.

◉ Transportation and Energy

Botswana lacks a well-developed transportation system. The main railway line from South Africa to Zimbabwe passes through the eastern part of Botswana. Branch lines serve the Selebi-Phikwe mining complex and the coal mines at Morupule.

Paved highways connect Gaborone and other important towns. Botswana has about 5,000 miles (8,047 km) of paved roads. More than 10,000 miles (16,093 km) of earth-and-sand routes also crisscross the country. The highway from Gaborone to Kazungula, Zambia—where the borders of Botswana, Namibia, Zambia, and Zimbabwe meet—is tarred, as is the Palapye-to-Serowe road. Relatively few Botswanans own cars. Most people travel by foot, bicycle, or animal-drawn vehicle.

The center of Botswana's air network is Sir Seretse Khama International Airport, which opened in 1984. From this international landing field in Gaborone, Air Botswana, Royal Swazi National Airways, and Zambia Airways operate regular services to South Africa, Zambia, and Zimbabwe. Regional airports and smaller airfields are located at all major population centers and tourist sites.

Except for coal and wood, Botswana lacks significant fuel sources. It does hold some natural gas, but these reserves have yet to be widely explored. The nation imports most of its petroleum from South Africa. The Morupule power station, located in northeastern

Botswana has a network of small airports, including Maun Airport, that reach into remote parts of the country. Maun Airport serves mostly tourists visiting the Okavango Delta and nearby game reserves.

Botswana, provides most of the nation's electrical energy. Experts are also exploring solar power as a source of energy.

The Future

A variety of factors affect Botswana's prospects for the future. For example, traditional landowning patterns and social structures favor members of the Batswana upper class. These age-old ways hold back economic output. Many citizens have a low standard of living. And the nation's single most valuable product—diamonds—depends heavily on the world market and fluctuating prices.

The nation also faces a great challenge in addressing HIV/AIDS. The disease's effect on Botswana has been massive. Much of the country's future will depend on the outcome of efforts to slow or stop the disease's spread.

But Botswana also boasts many strengths. One of its greatest assets is its stable political situation. Skilled in the complex politics of southern Africa, the country's leaders prepare to meet the challenges of social change and economic growth that lie ahead.

KEEPING IN TOUCH

Botswanans stay in touch in a variety of ways. The nation has more than 60,000 Internet users, as well as 80,000 personal computers. In addition, there are an estimated 800,000 cellular phone subscribers—more than five times the number of telephone lines in use.

Visit www.vgsbooks.com for links to websites with up-to-date information about Botswana's economy. Learn how Botswana is doing in its fights against poverty and HIV/AIDS.

CA. 48,000 B.C.	Early humans live in the area that will later become Botswana.
CA. A.D. 100	Bantu-speaking peoples begin migrating southward from central Africa.
1000–1250	Mining increases in the region.
CA.1300	Batswana people dominate Botswana in number.
EARLY 1600S	Batswana clans arriving in Botswana expand areas of settlement and trade.
1652	Boers join the Cape Colony.
1815	The Zulu warrior-king Shaka organizes an army to compete with the Batswana.
1817	Missionary Robert Moffat arrives in Cape Town.
1820s–1830s	The difaqane pushes many Batswana and other groups from their homes.
1835	The Afrikaner Great Trek takes place.
1848	Sechele I becomes a Christian.
1849	David Livingstone reaches Lake Ngami.
1862	Thomas Baines paints the baobabs then known as the Sleeping Sisters.
1885	The British tell the Batswana that their lands are under British protection. They name the area the Bechuanaland Protectorate.
1890s	Cecil Rhodes tries to gain control of Bechuanaland.
1895	Three Batswana kings travel to Great Britain to protest the proposed transfer of Bechuanaland to the British South Africa Company.
1910	The Union of South Africa is established. The British establish the Southern African Customs Union (SACU).
1914–1918	World War I is fought.
1919	The British form the Native Advisory Council (later the African Council).
1931	The Batswana join the Native Advisory Council.
1939	World War II breaks out.
1948	Seretse Khama marries Ruth Williams.
1960	The Bechuanaland Peoples' Party (BPP) is formed.

1962   The Bechuanaland Democratic Party (BDP) is formed.

1966   Botswana becomes independent, and the Republic of Botswana is established. Seretse Khama becomes its first president.

1967   Major diamond deposits are discovered in Botswana.

1968   The National Museum and Art Gallery opens in Gaborone.

1972–1979   Refugees from Rhodesia's civil war enter Botswana.

1980   Seretse Khama dies. Quett Masire succeeds him as president. Botswana competes in the Olympics for the first time at the Summer Olympics.

1982   The University of Botswana opens in Gaborone.

1984   The Sir Seretse Khama International Airport opens in Gaborone.

1985   The first case of AIDS in Botswana is reported.

1987   The first Maitisong Festival, showcasing the arts, takes place.

1991   The Mogwana Dance Troupe is formed.

1999   Voters elect Festus Mogae president.

2003   A San group begins a lawsuit against the Botswana government, demanding their right to remain in the Central Kalahari Game Reserve. A woman leads a Batswana group for the first time.

2006   The San win their court case.

2008   Ian Khama becomes president.

COUNTRY NAME Republic of Botswana

AREA 231,800 square miles (600,370 sq. km)

MAIN LANDFORMS Tsodilo Hills, Okavango River delta, Kalahari Desert

HIGHEST POINT Otse Mountain, 4,886 feet (1,489 m) above sea level

LOWEST POINT Junction of the Limpopo and Shashe rivers, 1,683 feet (513 m) above sea level

MAJOR RIVERS Chobe, Limpopo, Okavango, Shashe

ANIMALS antelope, bustards, crocodiles, elephants, flamingos, giraffes, hippopotamuses, lions, leopards, ostriches, pelicans, wildebeests, zebras

CAPITAL CITY Gaborone

OTHER MAJOR CITIES Francistown, Molepolole, Selebi-Phikwe, Serowe, Lobatse

OFFICIAL LANGUAGES English and Setswana

MONETARY UNIT Pula. 100 thebe = 1 pula.

BOTSWANAN CURRENCY

In 1976 Botswana introduced the pula. This new national currency replaced the South African rand that the nation had been using. Bills are available in denominations of 10, 20, 50, and 100 pula. Coins are minted in values of 5, 10, 25, and 50 thebe, as well as 1, 2, and 5 pula.

Each of Botswana's coins bears the nation's coat of arms on one side. On the other, each coin shows a native animal, such as zebras and rhinoceroses. The bills show political figures including presidents Seretse Khama and Festus Mogae and traditional chiefs. Some illustrations on banknotes highlight economic activities in Botswana, such as people tending cattle herds or inspecting diamonds.

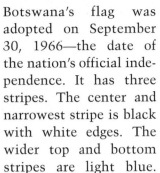

Botswana's flag was adopted on September 30, 1966—the date of the nation's official independence. It has three stripes. The center and narrowest stripe is black with white edges. The wider top and bottom stripes are light blue. The blue color represents water or rain—always a welcome sight in such a dry land. The black stripe and its white borders have a double meaning. They symbolize racial harmony and diversity, as well as representing the zebras that still roam the nation. Zebras are officially the national animal and also appear in the nation's coat of arms.

Botswana's national anthem was adopted when the nation became independent in 1966. Kgalemang Tumedisco Motsete (1900–1974) wrote the words and composed the music. Botswana's anthem is called "Fatshe leno la rona," or "Blessed Be This Noble Land." The English version captures the anthem's spirit while also rhyming. Here are the song's first verse and chorus in Setswana and English:

Fatshe leno la rona,
Ke mpho ya Modimo,
Ke boswa jwa borraetsho;
A le nne ka kagiso.

CHORUS:
Tsogang, tsogang! banna, tsogang!
Emang, basadi, emang, tlhagafalang!
Re kopaneleng go direla
Lefatshe la rona.

Blessed be this noble land,
Gift to us from God's strong hand,
Heritage our fathers left to us.
May it always be at peace.

CHORUS:
Awake, awake, O men, awake!
And women close beside them stand,
Together we'll work and serve
This land, this happy land!

For a link to a site where you can listen to Botswana's national anthem, "Fatshe leno la rona," visit www.vgsbooks.com.

LESEGO BILE (b. 1984) Born in Gaborone, Bile is Botswana's first female kwaito singer. Also known as Lesh, she knew from a young age that she wanted to be a musician. Her first album came out in 2006, and she has quickly become a popular star. In addition to making music, Bile has worked to help young people make good choices. She has worked with organizations that educate youth about drugs, HIV/AIDS, and other issues.

ISAAC CHIBUA (b. 1977) Isaac Chibua was born in Serowe. He knew from the time he was five years old that he wanted to be an artist. As a young man, he attended several arts workshops to hone his skills. He also worked as an art teacher, but creating his own art remained his passion. He has won several international awards for his painting and sculpture. Chibua's works have been on exhibit in nations including Namibia, South Africa, Finland, and China.

UNITY DOW (b. 1959) Dow was born in Mochudi, a town about 30 miles (48 km) northeast of Gaborone. She grew up to study law at the University of Botswana and Swaziland (later the University of Botswana) and also in Scotland. A successful lawyer, she went on to serve as a judge. In 1998 she became the first female judge on Botswana's High Court. She was one of the judges on the San case against the government regarding the Central Kalahari Game Reserve. Dow has also worked hard to improve human rights in her nation. She has focused especially on the rights of women and children. In addition, she is the author of several novels.

SERETSE KHAMA (1921–1980) Born in Serowe, Khama was a member of a Bangwato family with a long history of leadership. His grandfather, Khama III, had been a prominent kgosi. Although Seretse officially inherited the kgosi title when he was only four years old, he did not take on its duties until much later. As a young man, he went to college in South Africa and then in Great Britain, where he studied law. While in Great Britain, he married Ruth Williams. The couple went on to have three sons (two of them twins) and one daughter. Khama's marriage to a white woman was controversial, but he was a popular leader. Many Bangwato followed Seretse Khama as their kgosi. In addition, traditional Batswana leaders accepted him as an equal. And in 1966, Khama became the first president of independent Botswana. He remained the nation's leader until his death in 1980.

KHAMA III (ca. 1837–1923) Khama III was born in Mushu, a settlement about halfway between Gaborone and Selebi-Phikwe. He was the son of the Bangwato kgosi Sekgoma I. Khama and his father had many disagreements, including over the fact that Khama had become a Christian. Eventually, their differences led Khama to overthrow his father and take power as chief of the Bangwato people in 1875. Khama

III went on to become a popular leader, sometimes called Khama the Good. One of his most important political decisions came in 1895, when, along with the kgosis Bathoen and Sebele, Khama helped convince Great Britain to make Bechuanaland a protectorate. The goal of this move was protecting the area from the Boers and from rival African groups. Khama continued to reign as kgosi until his death in 1923. A few decades later, his grandson Seretse Khama would become Botswana's first president.

CALIFORNIA MOLEFE (b. 1980)

Molefe is a track athlete who has represented Botswana in many international events. The sprinter competed in the 2004 Summer Olympics in Athens, Greece. In 2006 Molefe won a silver medal in the 400-meter run at the International Association of Athletics Federations (IAAF) World Indoor Championships. The following year, he won a gold medal in the same event at the All-Africa Games. Molefe also holds the Botswanan record for the 400-meter run, with a time of 45.34 seconds.

MOSADI MURIEL SEBOKO (b. 1950)

Seboko was born in Ramotswa, a village about 20 miles (32 km) south of Gaborone. She was the first child of the Balete kgosi Mokgosi III. After attending college, she began working at a bank. She later became a manager there and worked at the same bank for more than twenty years. But after her father's death, she decided to try to become her people's new leader. With the support of women's groups, she argued that the position was her right, as Mokgosi III's oldest child. She also said that the time had come for a female chief. In 2001 traditional Balete elders chose Seboko as the group's new leader. Not all Balete were happy about the choice of a woman, and some challenged the decision. Nevertheless, Seboko officially became the first Batswana *kgosigadi* (female chief) two years later, in 2003. Thousands of people attended her coronation in Ramotswa. Her uncle Leabile Mokgosi said, "She is a born chief. She is calm, she is caring . . . she is intelligent."

RATSIE SETLHAKO (1899–1975)

Ratsie Setlhako was born in Mokgware, a village about 30 miles (48 km) south of Serowe. At times, he worked tending cattle. But he is remembered for being a master segaba player and one of his country's most beloved folk musicians. An elementary school named after Setlhako opened in Palapye in 2003.

GABORONE Botswana's capital city offers several key sights to the visitor. The National Museum and Art Gallery is a major attraction, with exhibits highlighting fine arts, traditional crafts, and more. Visitors stroll among the city's downtown skyscrapers, government buildings, and the University of Botswana's campus. The capital offers a wider variety of restaurants, shopping, and entertainment than smaller Botswanan cities. Sports lovers can catch a soccer game at the national stadium, and Kgale Hill offers a great view of the city. Gaborone also serves as a good base for visiting the nearby Mokolodi Nature Reserve, which is home to zebras, elephants, hippos, giraffes, and many other animals.

KALAHARI DESERT The Kalahari is a beautiful and sometimes harsh part of Botswana. The Central Kalahari Game Reserve is a major attraction and is home to many thousands of desert animals. Wildlife here includes springboks (a kind of antelope), wildebeests, hyenas, warthogs, cheetahs, and lions. The Kalahari village of D'kar is also worth a visit, as a center for traditional San arts and crafts. It hosts the Kuru San Traditional Dance Festival every August.

MAKGADIKGADI PANS NATIONAL PARK and **NXAI PAN NATIONAL PARK** These large national parks are a great place to camp. They offer dramatic landscapes, plenty of wildlife viewing, and the historic baobab stand known as Baines' Baobabs.

OKAVANGO DELTA One of the largest inland deltas in the world, the Okavango Delta is a natural wonder in a dry nation. Adventurous travelers can take a ride in a *mokoro*, a traditional dugout canoe paddled by a local guide. Lucky visitors might even see elephants splashing and bathing in the river's cool waters.

SEROWE This city in eastern Botswana is the historic home of Seretse Khama's family, and it holds several related sights. The Khama III Memorial Museum explores the Khama family history and is housed in one of the family's former homes. Serowe is also the site of the Khama Royal Cemetery.

TSODILO HILLS The San believe that spirits live in the Tsodilo Hills, and some legends say that humans were first created here. But most modern visitors come to the hills to see the ancient rock paintings. The site has four main areas, known as Female Hill, Male Hill, Child Hill, and North Hill. More than 4,500 illustrations lie in an area of about 8.5 square miles (22 sq. km). They range in age, with the oldest dating from about 2000 B.C. and others from as recently as A.D. 700 or later. Most are in red or white paint. They show images of ancient life and hunting, as well as a wide range of wildlife. Zebras, giraffes, lions, whales, penguinlike birds, and dancing human figures all appear on the rock faces.

apartheid: a policy of segregation and political and economic discrimination against nonwhites in the Republic of South Africa

Bantu: a family of languages spoken in central and southern Africa

brackish: mixed salt water and freshwater

clan: a large network of families whose members trace their history to a common ancestor

colony: a territory ruled and occupied by a foreign power

delta: the clay, silt, sand, or similar material at the mouth of a river that is deposited by running water, forming a triangular section of land

drought: a period, usually several months long, when a region receives very little or no precipitation. Droughts can have devastating effects on farming, as well as on freshwater supplies.

gross domestic product (GDP): a measure of the total value of goods and services produced within the boundaries of a country in a certain amount of time (usually one year), regardless of the citizenship of the producers

indigenous: native to a particular place

literacy: the ability to read and write a basic sentence. A country's literacy rate is one indicator of its level of human development.

missionary: a religious worker who works in a foreign country. Missionaries often attempt to convert people to their religion.

nomad: a person who travels from place to place seasonally, following game, or according to the needs of livestock, rather than living in a permanent home year-round. Traditionally, the San people were nomadic.

parliament: a national representative body with legislative power

protectorate: a country that is under the control, or authority, of another country

purchasing power parity (PPP): PPP converts a country's currency into "international dollars," making it possible to compare how much similar goods and services cost to the residents of different countries

savanna: a flat, almost treeless grassland

United Nations: an international organization formed at the end of World War II in 1945 to help handle global disputes. The United Nations replaced a similar, earlier group known as the League of Nations.

Selected Bibliography

Greenway, Paul. *Botswana*. Oakland: Lonely Planet Publications, 2001.
This travel guide provides visitors to Botswana with information on lodging, dining, and attractions, as well as offering an overview of the nation's geography, climate, and history.

Keene-Young, Robyn, and Adrian Bailey. *Okavango: A Journey*. Cape Town: Struik Publishers, 2006.
This richly illustrated book explores the Okavango Delta and its wildlife.

Main, Michael. *Botswana: A Quick Guide to Customs and Etiquette*. New York: Random House, 2007.
This title offers details about cultural expectations and habits in Botswana and provides tips on having good manners in the country.

McIntyre, Chris, and Simon Atkins. *Guide to Namibia and Botswana*. Chalfont Saint Peter, UK: Bradt, 1994.
In addition to travel information, this guide presents background about Botswana's history, culture, climate, and more.

New York Times Company. *The New York Times on the Web*. 2008.
http://www.nytimes.com (August 7, 2008).
This online version of the newspaper offers current news stories along with an archive of articles on Botswana.

Omer-Cooper, J. D. *History of Southern Africa*. Portsmouth, NH: Heinemann, 1994.
This book provides historical background for both Botswana and its neighbors in southern Africa.

PRB. "PRB 2007 World Population Data Sheet." *Population Reference Bureau*. 2007.
http://www.prb.org (August 7, 2008).
This annual statistics sheet provides a wealth of data on Botswana's population, birthrates and death rates, fertility rate, infant mortality rate, and other useful demographic information.

Routledge. *Europa World Year Book, 2007*. Vol. I. London: Europa Publications, 2007.
Covering Botswana's recent history, economy, and government, this annual publication also provides a wealth of statistics on population, employment, trade, and more.

Turner, Barry, ed. *The Statesman's Yearbook: The Politics, Cultures, and Economies of the World, 2007*. New York: Macmillan Press, 2006.
This resource provides concise information on Botswana's history, climate, government, economy, and culture, including relevant statistics.

UNICEF. "Botswana." *UNICEF: Information by Country*. 2008.
http://www.unicef.org/infobycountry/botswana.html (August 8, 2008).
This site from the United Nations agency UNICEF offers details about education, nutrition, and other demographics in Botswana.

U.S. Department of State. "Botswana." *U.S. Department of State: Country Reports on Human Rights Practices.* **2008.**
http://www.state.gov/g/drl/rls/hrrpt/2006/78720.htm (August 7, 2008).
This website is published by the U.S. State Department's Bureau of Democracy, Human Rights, and Labor. It provides a yearly update on the human rights situation within Botswana, including concerns about women's rights, treatment of the San people, and other issues.

World Health Organization. "Botswana." *World Health Organization: Countries.* **2008.**
http://www.who.int/countries/bwa/en/ (August 7, 2008).
This website provides a wealth of statistics and information on HIV/AIDS and other health issues in Botswana.

Africa: Explore the Regions: Southern Africa
http://www.pbs.org/wnet/africa/explore/southern/southern_overview.html
This PBS website introduces visitors to the people, geography, and environment of southern Africa. Hear a zebra bray, try out a regional recipe, and more.

BBC News—Africa
http://news.bbc.co.uk/2/hi/africa/
This news site provides a range of up-to-date information and archived articles about Botswana and the surrounding region.

CNN.com International
http://edition.cnn.com/WORLD/
Check CNN for current events and breaking news about Botswana, as well as a searchable archive of older articles.

Cornell, Kari. *Cooking the Southern African Way*. Minneapolis: Lerner Publications Company, 2005.
This cookbook presents a selection of recipes from Botswana and its surrounding region. Cooks in Botswana and throughout southern Africa use many of the same ingredients and methods to prepare meals.

Diouf, Sylviane A. *Kings and Queens of Southern Africa*. New York: Franklin Watts, 2000.
This book describes the lives and times of some of the major rulers who dominated southern Africa many years before Botswana became a nation.

Hamilton, Janice. *South Africa in Pictures*. Minneapolis: Twenty-First Century Books, 2004.
As Botswana's neighbor to the south and as another former British colony, South Africa shares many cultural and historical ties with Botswana. Read this book to learn more about this nation.

Jenkins, Martin. *Deserts*. Minneapolis: Lerner Publications Company, 1996.
This book explores deserts around the world, including the people, plants, and animals that live in these harsh areas.

Lonely Planet: Niger
http://www.lonelyplanet.com/worldguide/destinations/africa/botswana/
Visit this website for information about traveling to Botswana. You can also see images and learn some background information about the country at this site.

McCall Smith, Alexander. *The No. 1 Ladies' Detective Agency*. New York: Pantheon Books, 1998.
This mystery novel is set in Botswana and is the first title in a popular series. In 2007 a made-for-television movie based on the books was filmed in Botswana.

Parker, Linda. *The San of Africa*. Lerner Publications Company, 2002.
This book explores the history and culture of Africa's San people, many of whom live in Botswana.

Further Reading and Websites

Streissguth, Tom. *Namibia in Pictures*. **Minneapolis: Twenty-First Century Books, 2009.**
Learn more about Botswana's region of Africa with this title on Botswana's neighbor to the west.

vgsbooks.com
http://www.vgsbooks.com
Visit vgsbooks.com, the home page of the Visual Geography Series®. You can get linked to all sorts of useful online information, including geographical, historical, demographic, cultural, and economic websites. The vgsbooks.com site is a great resource for late-breaking news and statistics.

Waters, Bella. *Zambia in Pictures*. **Minneapolis: Twenty-First Century Books, 2009.**
Learn more about Botswana's region of Africa with this title on Botswana's neighbor to the north.

Woods, Michael, and Mary B. Woods. *Seven Natural Wonders of Africa*. **Minneapolis: Twenty-First Century Books, 2009.**
Discover seven beautiful natural wonders from across the African continent, including Victoria Falls in neighboring Zimbabwe.

Woods, Michael, and Mary B. Woods. *Seven Wonders of Ancient Africa*. **Minneapolis: Twenty-First Century Books, 2009.**
Explore seven places built by Africans in ancient times.

Captions for photos appearing on cover and chapter openers:

Cover: Boatmen travel down the Okavango River in *mokoros*, a type of traditional dugout canoe.

pp. 4–5 Cape buffalo wander across the Okavango River delta in northwestern Botswana.

pp. 8–9 The Kalahari Desert covers 70 percent of Botswana.

pp. 20–21 Early groups living in the Tsodilo Hills of northwestern Botswana created these rock paintings of animals.

pp. 38–39 A group of children crowd in for a picture outside of a school in Kasane, a town in the far north where Botswana meets Zambia, Zimbabwe, and Namibia.

pp. 46–47 Women prepare traditional food for a Botswanan harvest festival.

pp. 58–59 Workers polish diamonds at a new factory in Gaborone. Diamonds contribute significantly to Botswana's economy.